MW01047535

JUSTICE PREVAILS

Sandra Mae Brown

Best wishes
Sandra Brown
Hugs!

Copyright © 2013 by Sandra Mae Brown
First Edition – July 2013

ISBN
978-1-4602-2806-7 (Hardcover)
978-1-4602-2303-1 (Paperback)
978-1-4602-2304-8 (eBook)

All rights reserved.

No part of this publication may be reproduced in any form, or by any means, electronic or mechanical, including photocopying, recording, or any information browsing, storage, or retrieval system, without permission in writing from the publisher.

Produced by:

FriesenPress

Suite 300 – 852 Fort Street
Victoria, BC, Canada V8W 1H8

Www.friesenpress.com

Distributed to the trade by The Ingram Book Company

Table of Contents

A NOTE OF THANKS

I wish to thank my best friend, Gwen Nichols, for her interest and hard work and for helping me bring my story to light. From the very first day I met her, Gwen has made me feel like a somebody. She has supported me throughout this whole ordeal. Having her believe in me has meant more than words can say.

I also wish to thank Dr. Neil Shepherd for his support and understanding ear. Special thanks to Dr. Ross Martin for his long hours of hard work as he stood by me. I'd also like to thank the late Dr. Twomey and the staff at the Botwood Cottage Hospital. They saved my life.

I'd like to say thanks to the McCarthys of Grand Falls-Windsor, Newfoundland. They showed a frightened little girl that she was loved. To my special friend, Karen, and her late husband, Stanley, thank you for opening your hearts and making me feel special, and to their daughters for looking up to me as their "Aunt Sandra."

To my long list of friends, many thanks to you all for your words of kindness! To the Canning family, thank you for accepting me as one of your own.

To my three children—Charlene, Hannah, and Curt Douglas—and my grandchildren: you have been my source of strength. I love you all very much.

PROLOGUE

A Message to the World

My name is Sandra M. Brown. I live in St. Catharine's, Ontario. I am a survivor of child abuse. Both my parents were eventually tried and convicted of this unspeakable crime. For ruining my life, they each served close to a two-year prison term in the early 1990's.

Why am I writing this now? My hope is that, by sharing my experiences, I can prevent similar things from happening to other children, so that they won't have to go through what I had to endure.

My writing is based on facts established in court, and especially the factual content of medical reports. Court documents, which I will quote from later in the book, in their own way chronicle the events of all the horror I remember living as a child. While this may seem a cold and clinical approach, it's the only way I can tell my story.

I have been trying to write this story for fifteen years. It has been a long and arduous journey. I have come a long way in doing so. I left school with a grade three education. Over the years, with the help of my friends, my children, my grandchildren, and those with whom I shared work and neighbourhood experiences, I have learned to read and write enough to see my dream of sharing my story become a reality.

My goal in writing this book is to send a message to the world and draw public attention and action to the issues of child abuse.

For the children who cannot speak for themselves, I want to tell their parents, "Mommy and Daddy, don't hurt me!"

CHAPTER ONE
MEETING MY FAMILY

Here is my story, especially the story of the unusual difficulties of my childhood years. I feel that it needs to be told. I hope I can help others who are living a life of pain because of the child abuse they experienced. Of course, there are no words that will take away one's painful past or the sleepless nights.

Quite often my thoughts stray back to the unhappy days of my childhood. It's true that life was much simpler then for most people, but for me it was a private hell. I can't remember ever being happy. I keep hoping the past will go away. Unfortunately, right now, it's ever-present in my mind. An inner supply of courage is my only strength for carrying on.

From infancy to age seventeen I was physically and mentally abused by my mother and father, Breta and Theodore Brown, in small towns in central Newfoundland. Somehow I have blocked out the first four years of my life, or maybe I was just too young to remember. But medical records dating from 1961 to 1971 have provided me with insight into those years.

On September 25, 1961, at the age of thirty-one months, I was admitted to the Botwood Cottage Hospital in Newfoundland and treated for diarrhea and vomiting.

Medical records indicate I was very quiet and weak, and suffering from gross abdominal distension and dehydration. There were bruises on my face, forehead, and chin. My eyes were sunken. My condition was treated as gastroenteritis. After a few days in the hospital, with medical attention and an intravenous drip, I improved considerably and was released to the custody of my parents.

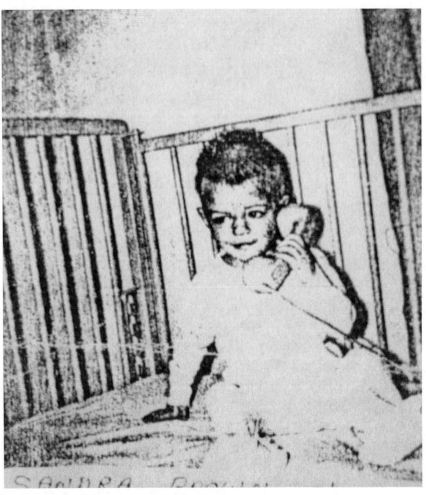

This photo was taken by one of the nurses at Botwood Cottage Hospital back in 1963. I will always be grateful to Dr. Martin and the staff at the Botwood Cottage Hospital.

Two years later I was again admitted to the Botwood hospital, in a semi-conscious state, and was this time examined by Dr. Hugh Twomey. His report states there were sores on my head and faint bruising on my cheeks. Dr. Twomey also stated that my skin was covered with caked dirt. At age four I weighed only sixteen pounds and ten ounces.

On September 18, 1963, two months after my first visit to Dr. Twomey, I was again admitted to the hospital for a period of approximately five weeks with sores, a bruised face, sunken eyes, and scratches on my abdomen. Dr. Twomey said that in some ways I looked like a dying inmate of a concentration camp. Approximately five weeks later I was released and placed in a foster home.

I then lived for about six months with Mr. And Mrs. McCarthy of Windsor, Newfoundland. I remember just a few things about that time in my life. One was when the teapot broke on the stove. I was afraid and started to cry when I saw the loose tea leaves run down the side of the white stove. Right away I assumed that it was my fault and that I was in for a beating. To my amazement Mrs. McCarthy cuddled me and said it wasn't my fault. I don't remember ever being cuddled before. Until that day I didn't know what the feeling of love was.

A treasured memory of this time was when an old man wearing a hat gave me a quarter. I ran to the store as he watched me through the window to make sure I was safe going and coming across the street. I recall buying candy. The sweets were shaped like little red christmas bells with marshmallow inside. I held on tight to this little brown bag.

It was the first time I'd been given a treat. I don't remember if this man was Mr. McCarthy or some neighbour visiting that day, but I surely was happy to get the candy. It didn't matter who the man was. The important thing is he left this little girl with a good memory from her childhood. That incident occurred over forty-seven years ago, but I still remember it like it was yesterday.

Another memory of my life with the McCarthys was playing in the snow on a warm winter day with two boys who were much older and bigger than I was. I don't remember if they were foster children or the McCarthys' sons. They were showing me how to make angels in the snow. As I looked to both sides and saw the wings, I was so happy and wanted to make more. But one of the boys said, "No, we have to go inside now. It'll be getting dark soon. We need to get ready for dinner."

I was having so much fun in the snow that afternoon and didn't want the day to end. That was my first time making something so beautiful, clean, and pure. I was sad when the sun came out and melted the snow. With disappointment I watched as my angel wings disappeared. Little did I suspect that, like the angel wings, my life with the McCarthys was also fleeting.

Mrs. McCarthy was very sweet. After she took my coat off and put it on the line to dry, she then took my hand and walked with me to the table where hot chocolate and cookies were waiting to warm my body and soothe my disappointment over the loss of my snow angels.

My happy days with the McCarthys soon ended when the social worker came and took me and all my things with her one hot summer day. Sadly I said goodbye to Mrs. McCarthy. The social worker drove off with me to return me to my life of hell. She had no idea what those people were capable of doing or just what was in store for me. All she knew was that they were churchgoing folks and well-known in the little town of Norris Arm North.

I didn't understand why I was being taken from my loving foster family and returned to a home and parents who didn't want anything to do with me. For six brief months my life had been protected and nurtured. I didn't understand why the social worker would take me from a home where I was fed and cared for and bring me to this place with all its horrendous treatment.

I remember that day as if it were yesterday. The social worker held my hand as we were walking toward a dirty and rundown old house. I couldn't understand why she was bringing me to this place. I had been so happy with the McCarthy family. Theirs was the nearest thing I had ever had to a real home. I had thought I'd be there forever. No one had given me any indication that this would not be the case.

So why was this lady bringing me here? I didn't know anyone here. But as we got to the door, there was a little boy playing with a bike. It was turned upside down, and he was spinning the wheel around and around. I had no idea who he was and didn't recall seeing him before. The social worker introduced this boy as my brother Joey. Then a girl came to open the door. The lady asked if I knew who it was. Again I replied no. She said, "That's your sister Patty."

As we went into the house, I looked up. There was a large woman standing in the kitchen. The social worker introduced her as my mother. I had no recollection of her.

But I was instantly terrified of this woman called "Mother." I didn't want to stay there. I remember grabbing onto the social worker's leg and pushing her toward the door. I was frantic to get out of there.

"It's okay, Sandra," The social worker said. "That's your mother. She's not going to hurt you anymore. Everything is going to be okay."

After a short visit with this woman whom she called my mother, the social worker took my things out of the car. She said her goodbyes and drove away, leaving me standing in front of the filthy shack.

Later that afternoon I went outside to play with my new brother and sister, Joey and Patty. They were nice to me. We had fun playing beside a big rock. Then I saw a man walking toward us. My mother asked me if I knew who he was. I thought it was my father. Mother said, "No, that's your grandfather. Your father is away working. He'll be home on the weekend."

There was something about this woman called Mother I didn't like. She left me feeling so cold. I remember looking down the long pathway toward the road, hoping the social worker would come back for me. But she never did. She came in the days after that, but only to visit.

Within days of my return to this family, the beatings started again. I was being beaten every day and night, and I couldn't understand why. What was I doing wrong? What made Mother hate me so much? I was the only child who suffered at the hands of my mother and father. I was number two in a family of nine children. Why was I the only one who was abused? The question continues to haunt me.

In the earlier years it was just me, my brother Joey, and my sister Patty whom I can remember well. I remember hearing them crying when Mother would yell and order them to hold me down as she laid a beating on me. They were just children and couldn't understand why Mother would do this to me. At the same time they feared to disobey her, hoping with everything in them that she wouldn't do the same to them.

I remember my brother Joey crying as he pleaded with me not to cry because it would make Mom mad. "If you don't cry," He begged me, "maybe she won't beat you again."

Joey was too young to understand how much pain I was in and how badly my body hurt from the beatings. He was just trying to save me from more abuse and was convinced that if I stopped crying, it would all go away.

My sister Patty would hug me and wash the blood from my body and try to stop the bleeding. She would say, "God is going to come and take us out of here. But you have to be good, okay? Try real hard to stop crying." I would say okay and ask when God was going to come for us. Patty would say, "Soon. He's coming soon."

With big tears rolling down my face, I would ask Patty, "Why is Mother hurting me like this?" I'd ask, "How come she's not beating you and Joey?"

Patty would tell me it was because she and Joey didn't cry all the time like I did.

I would reply, "I don't want to live here. When am I going back home?"

Patty would remind me sadly, "But that's not your real home. You were just staying there because you were very sick and Mother couldn't take care of you."

I remember my mother getting very upset one time

When she noticed that I had messed in my clothes. But I was too little to sit on the bucket they used as a toilet, and I was not allowed to go outside to the outhouse. So there I was in trouble again.

Most of the time I would walk around with my head down in fear of making eye contact with my mother because even that would upset her, and every time she got mad I was in for a beating. Mother would continue to beat me until she had no energy left in her body. When the beating was over, I would be very weak and unable to walk. I couldn't understand why my parents would beat me and make me go hungry. There was always lots of food for the other children in that house.

Most nights I was not able to lie on my back to sleep because it was so sore. I was always terrified. Mother would yell at me and say, "Shut your mouth or you'll get it again." I was not allowed to cry. If Mother heard me, she would beat me even harder than before. There was just no way out.

I remember many times when my Grandfather Brown came to our house and tried to stop Mother from beating me. When he went home, Mother would be furious with him. She would take it out on me even worse than before. She would send me back to the dark little room they sent me to for punishment without anything to eat or drink.

Some nights people would come to visit. That would make me happy because, as long as they were there, Mother would not hit me. Whenever we had visitors, Mother wouldn't say anything to me, but she would give me that cold look of hers. I knew from the look in her eyes that I was in for a beating after the visitors had gone.

I remember thinking to myself: How can I get to sleep before they leave? Maybe Mother won't beat me tonight because I'm still hurting from the beating I got today. But then later at night, when the visitors were gone home, Mother would pull me out of a deep sleep and punish me because, in her mind, something had gone wrong, or maybe she would notice some cookies were missing when she had set the table for her guests. Sometimes I would hear the visitors ask about me and ask where I was. Mother would reply by saying, "She's in bed, sick."

I remember sometimes waking up and being in a lot of pain but unable to move my body because my feet and my hands were tied down. There was also something tied tight around my mouth so I couldn't talk or call out for help. One time I remember opening my eyes and seeing a pink scarf wrapped around my left hand. Both my feet were tied down with a piece of rope. I was lying in a crib that had no mattress or blankets, just a few old coats that were all smelly with my body waste. It was all over the wall where the crib was placed in the room. I was left in this filthy condition almost every day and night ... until they started putting me in the little Black room.

The other children in this house got fed and washed and had their hair combed. They got to play with toys. When I had first come home to live with this family, I had had lots of toys like games, puzzles, and dolls. I just loved my dolls so much. I would talk to them and tell them, "I'm going to look pretty just like you someday." I would think to myself that maybe if I was pretty my family would love me, like I loved my dolls. Maybe Mother wouldn't beat me anymore, and she would feed me like the other children.

Within days of my returning home to this family, everything I had, like my pretty dresses, bows for my hair, shoes, dolls, puzzles, and games, was taken from me and given to Patty and Joey. I would cry because they got to play with my toys and I wasn't allowed to even touch them. One time I reached out as Patty was holding my doll in her arms. I just wanted to touch her pretty dress. But Patty yelled as she pulled the doll away and said, "Get your shitty fingers of my doll!" My beautiful dolls were now my sister's. I never got to hold them again. The other children got to go outside and play every day with the other children that lived nearby. I wasn't allowed to have playtime.

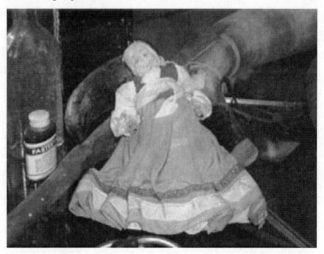

This is a photo of my doll that was taken from me and given to my sister.

I was now living in a dark, cold, smelly world with no way out and no one to turn to for help. I remember smelling bad and being very dirty all the time. My father was not much help when it came to protecting me in any way from the hands of Mother. He did whatever it took to make Mother happy. Most of the time he didn't even stop to ask what it was all about or what I had done wrong to deserve a beating. He just didn't care.

How bad could I have been for them to hate me so much? What was wrong with me? Why were they treating me this way? Why was I the only one who had to go without food or water to drink?

Sunday was the lord's Day, and we would attend church three times. When morning service was over, we would return home, and the family would enjoy a cooked meal with oven-baked chicken. After the meal was over, it was time for Sunday school. The teachers talked about Jesus and all the good things God would do for us. If we were good and kept coming back to church and lived for God, one day we would live with Him in Heaven. Sunday nights would be a time to sing praises unto the lord. People would stand up and tell of all the good things God had done for them.

When Mother stood to her feet and shouted about the glory of God, I would look up and say in a low voice, "God, can you keep her the way she is now?" Mother was a very pretty lady when she was all dressed up for church. She had lovely hair and pretty dresses, most of them made by her own hands. I loved her beautiful hats and shoes.

There was just something about Mother. She was a beauty who would light a room up when she walked into it. She was very caring and giving toward others. Her smile was so welcoming. I wanted to believe in my heart that she was a beautiful person. But then I sat alone on the floor of that Black room and listened to her yelling and throwing things around the house because she was in such a state of outrage.

I wished that every day could be Sunday because I liked what Mother became on the Lord's Day.

Mother was always more than willing to give a helping hand to anyone who needed help. To others, she seemed to be always happy and to have a really good spirit about her. I remember her being gone until late hours at night to help neighbours or fellow churchgoers. If Father wasn't home, we did things for ourselves. The house was so cold and dirty all the time. As a child, I thought it was a normal way to live.

At the age of six I made myself believe that there was something wrong with me, that somehow I was the reason for Mother being this way. Night after night I would pray that God would help me be a good girl and make me pretty like my sister Patty. Inside I felt dirty, like an old used doll that no one wanted.

Some nights my face would be wet with tears. There were nights when I would sob but no tears would come. I wanted Mother to feel my pain. Every night I would get on my knees and pray, "God, make Mother feel my pain, and somehow make her understand that I am hurting, that I am hungry and so cold." Still, each day things got worse in that house. I would think that maybe God hadn't heard my prayer the night before. Little by little, as time went on, I started giving up hope of ever making it out of that house alive.

Life went on, and so did the abuse. When I was six, I was moved from the dirty, wet, smelly crib to a dark hole in the wall. Inside this room it was pitch Black. I couldn't see a thing. This place became my world. My eyes became so accustomed to the dark that, when the time came for me to start school, I found myself blinking and closing my eyes often. The brightness of the outside world bothered me so much that I even had trouble looking up and seeing what the teacher had on the Blackboard. While my classmates were busy writing it all down on paper, I was still trying to see what was on the board. Everything was so bright outside the walls of that room. It was so dark in there. I remember at times moving around and feeling my way to the walls, trying to pull my body off the cold floor to keep warm through the night. But I was too weak and would fall back down again.

CHAPTER TWO
THE BLACK ROOM

While I was curled up in this little prison, I would often hear my mother setting the table, and I would wonder if maybe today they would bring me something to eat. I felt like a caged animal that was rarely fed. The best I could hope for was to hear Mother telling my sister to "take this in to the Other Thing." I was no longer called by my name, Sandra.

My sister was afraid to open the door to this small room, fearing I would attack her for the little food she brought to me. From the time I was five until I turned eight years old, most of my life was spent in a dark closet. There was no window or even a bed. It was just a small, dark room. I didn't know night from day because it was so Black inside. I would sit on the wooden floor, cold and hungry, as hour after hour passed. I was now just the Other Thing that no one wanted.

Day after day I would wonder if, maybe today, they would call me to come and sit at the table with them to eat. I wanted so much to be at the family table with everyone else and feel that I belonged. Days turned into months and months into years.

Anyone who knew about my situation was silent, including me. There was big talk throughout the town about the little Brown girl. Many thought I didn't exist.

They had never seen me. Until the time I attended school, most townspeople thought I was a story made up by fanciful children, like a ghost story.

My little Black room was so small that I couldn't even stand up and walk around. It was just a spot where they kept junk. There I was, alone, shivering in this cold, dark room. Night after night, through the winter months, I would sit on my hands to keep them warm, knowing by morning they would be numb.

If I was lucky, Mother would let me out to clean up the dishes. Maybe I'd get to eat the leftovers on the plates. Just like a rat scouring for food, I'd put it in my mouth as fast as I could and hope Mother wouldn't see me doing it. When she allowed me to eat, it was just a slice of bread with butter. Sometimes I didn't even get to eat it all. Mother would get outraged and order me, "Get in that goddamn room as fast as you can, and don't show your face out here anymore tonight!"

At first I was afraid of being inside the Black room. But as the months went by, it became life for me, the only place I felt safe. Some nights, when it was real cold, I would curl up and hold my body tight to keep myself warm and hope that I wouldn't die by morning. In the day Mother would pull me out to do the housecleaning. There was always lots of that to do. She would yell at me because I wasn't moving as fast as she thought I could, but I always did my best. I wanted so much to make her happy.

I would think to myself: Why can't she see that I'm just a little girl, and this is a lot of hard work for me to do? After the inside work was done, then came the outside work. It had to be done by us kids because at this time Father was working away from home a lot. He would leave Monday morning and come home Friday night. My brother, sister, and I had to get wood to keep the house warm for the family. After that was done, we had to bring water from the well.

We didn't like the days when it was time for Mother to wash the dirty clothes. It took her all day to get it done, and we were all day bringing water to keep the old wringer washer going. My brother and sister were lucky because, at the end of the day, they got to eat a real meal and got a warm bed to sleep in. But I was given a slice of bread and nothing more. If I was very lucky, I got a cup of hot tea to go with the bread. That piece of bread would be my dinner. After a hard day's work I would be sent back into the room and told to stay there.

People talked and went on with their lives, as the little girl suffered alone in silence, knowing that any moment could be her last. The rest of the family slept peacefully in their warm beds while she shivered in the cold.

At night I lay helpless in the cold, dark room, listening to the sound of the wind as it whistled through the cracks in the floorboards and never knowing when my next meal or slice of bread would be. Sometimes it would be as long as three days before they fed me. No bread or water. Nothing. I would get sick from being so hungry. Sometimes I would give up hope of ever making it out alive.

Once, when Mother had left the house and Father was outside getting wood, Patty opened the door and let me out of the room. My eyes caught what looked like a piece of chocolate cake on the kitchen floor. I was so hungry that I grabbed it as fast as I could and put it in my mouth. To my horror, it wasn't cake but a piece of body excrement. It still makes me sick to think of how desperate I was for food. There were times that I ate my own waste because I was so hungry. I knew deep inside that I would never be a part of this family because I was just the Other Thing that belonged in a small Black room alone.

The sound of Mother's voice and her footsteps made me so afraid. The look in her eyes told me I was in trouble. I received beatings every day and most every night. Even if I was sick, they still beat me for some reason.

Many nights Father would drag me out of the room by the hair of my head and order me to get my clothes off, even my underwear. I would stand in front of him with not a thing on as I shivered with fear. I would hope that he would just slap me around with his hand and not use the belt because at least the hands were a little easier on my body. I think that in his sick mind this was his way of protecting me from Mother. He felt that if he was the one to lay a beating on me, it would be much easier than if Mother was the one doing the beating.

I remember a terribly disturbing incident involving my father. Mother had gone out for a while and Father let me out of the closet. When my baby sister started to cry, he asked me to change her diaper. I tried my best to soothe her, but I was just a seven-year-old girl and didn't know how to care for a baby. I picked her up, put her on the sofa, and began to remove the pins from her diaper, trying real hard not to stick the pins in her. She was very messy, so I attempted to clean her up the best way I knew how. Then I brought her back to the crib.

Father asked me if the baby was clean. I replied in a soft, shivering voice, "Yes, Dad, she's clean." At that, he walked to the crib and, looking at me, said, "If she's not clean, you're going to get this," Meaning his belt. He removed her diaper and then took off his belt, screaming, "Does that look clean to you?"

I shook with terror as he grabbed my hair and demanded I lick the baby's bottom clean. I was so frightened! As he pushed my face down into her bum, I felt so dirty. But did my father care? No! He just beat me when I was finished and then joked about it.

As I sat on the floor of that cold, dark room, I kept telling myself that one day that woman—the social worker— was going to come back to get me out of this place. But she never did. Where did she go, I wondered. She was my only hope of ever getting out of there.

I remember her coming to talk to Mother and Father. Before she got to the door, I was always threatened not to say a word about anything. "Just sit on that chair and not a word out of that goddamn mouth of yours," Mother would warn me. The visits were very short. Mother was always so sweet to the social worker, like a real angel. Father never once said a word. Mother did all the talking. I sat there on the chair, just hoping the social worker would ask if she could take a look at my body to see if there were any marks. I thought if she could see how my body was covered with bruises and dried blood, she would waste no time in getting me out of there. She would take me back home to the McCarthy house.

One time the social worker came to visit in the winter. I remember that day very well because it was snowing heavily, and the wind was blowing hard. My father opened the door to help her into the house. They sat down at the table beside the window and began to talk about me. My mother assured the worker that I was well cared for just like the other children in the house. I remember the worker saying, "Mrs. Brown, if I find out you've laid a beating on Sandra or mistreated her in any way, you'll lose her and never get her back again."

I sat there on the chair that day, just like every other time she came for a visit, and spoke not a word about the beatings that went on in our home day after day and night after night. I was hoping that maybe someday she would come and see that I was being beaten and left without food for days at a time.

As time went on, I realized that her visits to our house were over and all my hopes of being taken from that home were now gone.

*

Mother always attended church social events. She was one of the best Sunday school teachers. All the children loved Mrs. Brown and wanted her to teach them. I would sit there Sunday after Sunday and watch her as she helped the other children with their work. She was so soft-spoken and sweet to them. I remember wondering why she couldn't be like that to me. I knew it was just wishful thinking.

After church was over, all the people would give each other hugs and talk about how God was going to send blessings and help those in need and feed the hungry. I remember thinking to myself that when we got home from church, God was going to tell my mother to feed me just as she fed the others in our home. But every time she came home from church, she would turn into another person and start yelling, screaming, and throwing things around the house. It was like a never-ending nightmare.

I loved it when visitors came to our house because it was so cheerful, even if only for a few hours. I would watch as Mother set the table to give them lunch. She'd put out luncheon meat, salads, cake, cookies—all those goodies that I never got.

Mother was well-known for her baking. The cakes and cookies she made would make your mouth water. Who could forget those thick lemon pies, golden brown on top, and the thick brownies covered with nuts? Or the homemade fudge and the cinnamon rolls that my brother and sister took to school for snacks? Or the custard and Jell-O she would have on the table for Sunday after-noon desserts?

At night, when they were all asleep, I would find my way out of the dark room and tiptoe my way to the table in the dark. I'd get a piece of bread and run back into the room again and eat it as fast as I could. The cakes and cookies were always put away somewhere, and there was no time to try and find them, so I'd grab some bread and race back to the room. Night after night I would get caught.

When that happened, both Mother and Father would beat me until the blood came. After the beating was over, they would pull me by the hair around the house. Many times I saw my hair on the floor and I would wonder if there was any left on my head. They would be screaming and yelling at me all the time. My father would shout, "If that don't teach you a lesson, the next time you'll get the cat-o'nine-tails!" He'd go on to describe it. He would say, "Now look at me and listen to what I have to tell you. The cat-o'nine-tails is nine whips that are strapped to a stick. You'll be tied face down on four poles with not a stitch of clothes on your body, and you will get whipped nine times."

After he was done telling me about this threatened punishment, I would then be pushed back into the Black room. He would always remind me of this, every night, with that wicked smile on his face. "Now don't forget what I told you about the cat-o'-nine-tails."

My mother's words were more menacing: "I'll kill you. I won't leave a bit of you to be seen," She would say, or "I'll give you scars to carry to your grave."

Sometimes Mother would make me watch as they ate their meals. After they were done, I was told to get the dishes washed as fast as I could and get into the dark room without food. One day she caught me taking a piece of salt beef fat from the garbage. As I put it in my mouth, she grabbed me by the hair and dragged me around the house, pulling as hard as she could.

Another time Mother threw a piece of wood and hit me in the back of the head. I remember Father yelling to her that she could have killed me this time. Mother just stood there unmoved. Father worked fast, trying to stop the bleeding. The blood was running down my head so fast that it felt like someone was pouring warm water down on my head. I was not taken to the hospital for this injury, nor did I go to school for a long time because they didn't want anyone to know about the scar on my head. Father kept cleaning it with warm water and dabbing it with myrrh that he got from the fir trees. "That's better than any stitches the doctors will give you, my dear," He'd say.

There were times when my mother would use any object she could get her hands on to beat me. It didn't matter to her how big it was. Sometimes she would continue the beating until I would vomit. Some of the objects she used were extension cords, broom handles, sticks of wood and horsewhips. No matter how much they beat me, I was never allowed to cry.

Once I vomited on my clothes and was left in that filthy condition so long the vomit turned to mould. My sister Patty was ordered to strip me down before Mother whipped me with the belt again. After the beating was over, I was to go back into the dark room. There was not even a bucket for me to use as a toilet. I sat and slept in my own body waste. Throughout the whole ordeal I kept saying to myself, over and over, that my big brother would be coming for me soon. But now, looking back, I realize that there was no big brother. He existed only in my mind.

Another memory I have is of Mother cutting my hand with a knife at the dinner table when I reached for a second piece of bread. Blood ran from my fingers. I was then ordered to place both hands on the table while Mother continuously beat them with a stick. My sister said, "Mom, look at the blood! Sandra's hand is full of blood." Mother said, "I'll give the likes of that, her reaching across the table like that in this house! I'll kill the goddamn thing. She won't reach across the table ever again." There are marks on my body that I'll carry to my grave, just as Mother always told me they would.

More than thirty years have passed since I left my mother's house, but I still remember details like it was yesterday. The screaming, the yelling, and the hunger pangs remain etched in my memory, and I'll never forget the beatings and the cold nights either. Sometimes the memories are like a war going on in my head. I'll tell myself at night that what happened in that house was just a bad dream, but every morning I open my eyes and the scars are there to remind me that it did happen. Then I remember all too well how hungry and cold I was as a child, never knowing when I'd be given food. Sometimes it was as long as a week before I got anything to eat or drink.

On my way home from school I would rummage through neighbours' garbage. I'd find bottles with peanut butter, jam, or cheese spread. I'd clean them out with my hands and eat it. The best I could hope for at home, if anything, was a small piece of dry bread.

Most evenings, after school, I returned home with the other children. They were fed and given time out to play with their toys. But for me there wasn't any playtime. Most days Joey or Patty had a report to give my mother about the things I did going to and coming from school. Most of their reports were about me picking up things from the ground to eat. They were just little, like me, and didn't understand the depths of my hunger and to what lengths

I would go for something to eat. Unlike me, they got their meals every day and snacks before going to bed.

I would pick up dirty apple cores, banana skins, dirty candy ... anything at all. I remember many times picking up candy that was full of little rocks or sand, putting it in my mouth to suck off the dirt and spitting it on the ground. I would close my eyes and suck on that candy. "Mmm! It's so sweet!" I loved the taste of that candy. The few minutes it took to eat that candy helped me forget the beating that was waiting for me at home.

Mother was always waiting there with a stick in her hand. Sometimes I got beaten for walking home from school too slowly, but unlike the other children in school, home was the last place I wanted to go. I remember many times walking home with the wind blowing hard in my face and hoping that it would blow me so far away that I would never be seen again. Going home every day to the beatings, the Black room, and nothing to eat was worse than a nightmare because nightmares are gone in the morning. But for me it was real life, and I was trapped with no way out.

You may wonder if I feared dying as a child. The answer is that every day I hoped with all my being to die in my sleep or get hit with a car as I walked to or from school. In the fall of the year all the men in the little town would let their horses out to run free. The horses would all run together like wild mustangs. I remember many times thinking, while coming and going from school, that if I got in the way of the horses, they would just run over my body and kill me, and that might be a good thing.

As I wondered into their path, Patty would pull me back and say, "Sandra, those horses will kill you if you don't get out of the way. Now don't do that again!" Sometimes she'd tell Mother what had happened, how I would get in the way of the stampeding horses, and then I would get beaten for that. Mother would yell and say that's how stupid I was, and that I'd never amount to anything in life.

I never told my sister or anyone else that I wished to die at the young age of six. I thought death was a way out. I would go to live with God and his angels. In church they talked a lot about when you die and go to Heaven. There would be no pain, no fighting, and no children going hungry. You would never be cold in Heaven. You'd walk on streets paved with gold, and Jesus would never leave you. I just wanted to die and go to live with Jesus and walk with the angels, so that no one would ever hurt me again.

But time went on and so did the beatings, night after night and day after day. Nothing ever changed in our house. Mother abused me in every way possible, and there was no way out. I had nowhere to turn.

I dared not look to my father for protection because, in my mother's eyes, he was just a nobody. He did whatever she told him to do, and he never once stood up to her. In many ways he was like a little boy. He would jump to his feet every time she told him to do something. Many times he would pick me up off the floor by my ears. Holding me high over his head, he'd toss my tiny body across the room like I was an old rag doll. He never once took time to ask questions about what I did wrong or why Mother was so upset. He just assumed it was my doing when he heard Mother's voice screaming, "I'll kill the goddamn thing if I get my hands on it. I won't leave a bit of it to be seen." Father would then raise his work-booted foot and kick me back into the cold, Black room, shouting at the top of his voice, "Don't show your face out here anymore this goddamn night, and don't let me hear one sound out of your mouth."

It didn't matter to them how much pain I was in or how sick I would get from the beatings. I was never allowed to cry. Father would sit on the chair and say, "Now get over here to me," And I would walk toward the chair where he was sitting. In a loud voice he would tell me to get my clothes off. "everything!" He would say. As I stood before him, naked, I remember thinking that I hoped they'd kill me this time. Grabbing me by the hair, he'd pull my face down into his legs. Holding my head tightly between his knees, he'd yell at my brother and sister to each take a leg and hold on real tight. "I want to make sure this Thing don't get away," He'd say.

He'd then tell my mother, "Now give it to her with everything you got in you, and don't stop until there's no life left." Mother would come down on me so hard I could feel the skin rip open with every blow of the whip. I could feel Joey and Patty's tears on my legs as they held them tight. They fought so hard to hold me down. They didn't want to, but they were so afraid. I can still hear their voices like an echo from afar: "She's going to die."

My sister screamed, "Mom, stop! You're going to kill her. Look at all the blood!" By this time my body was numb. I was, for a brief time, pain-free. Before I passed out, I wondered foggily if Mother had indeed killed me and this was Heaven.

Exhausted, Mother would stop, and they would let me go. I could feel my bloody body drop to the floor. I lay there, lifeless, too weak to pick myself up. I could feel someone kicking me. The next thing I remember is my sister putting a cool rag on my back.

I was so sore. It hurt so much. "Don't cry," She said in a soft voice. "Mom and Dad are sleeping. If they hear you crying, they will beat you again." My sister helped me up off the floor and held me in her little arms. She rocked me back and forth, trying to make me feel better. But it hurt so much. Even her gentle touch was excruciating. I could hear my little brother as he tiptoed into the dark room, bringing bread and water.

Patty fed me. I could feel Joey's little hand touch my arm as he pleaded with me to stop crying. "We don't want to wake Mom and Dad," He cautioned, "because they'll get real mad again."

The other kids went to school the next day, but I had to stay home because Mother didn't want anyone to see the marks on my body. She called the school and told my teacher that I would not be in school for a few days because I was sick. Days after this beating I was sent back to school with Mother's warning not to say a word to anyone. If they asked why I'd been out of school, I was to tell them I'd had a cold.

Sometimes the children in school would pull my skirt up and look at the marks on my body and ask, "Did your mother do that?" I would just shake my head and say no. Sometimes I would tell them that I'd fallen and hurt myself or that I'd bumped into the door at home.

I don't know if anyone outside our home knew about the dark room that I was kept in. My sisters and brother never said a word about it to anyone. The little, dark room was somewhere in the corner of a bedroom. The house was very small with just two bedrooms, one for Mother and Father, and the other for the children. Back at that time there were six of us children: five girls and one boy, Joey. The other children all slept in one big bed. I was to sleep, eat, and live in that little dark hole in the wall. As for knowing anything else about the house, such as what colour it was or how many other rooms there were, I don't know because I was only allowed out of the dark room when Mother ordered me to do things. I would do my work as fast as I could. I never took the time to look around for fear of upsetting Mother.

The first day of my return to this family, I do remember seeing the colour dark green. That was the colour of the cupboard doors where Mother was standing. We had no running water, and going to the well for water was one of the things I loved to do as a child. It was a way for me to get food. My grandparents made sure of that, when they could, without Mother knowing. They knew if Mother found out that they had fed me, I would get a beating, so they would tell me to eat fast. And you can be sure I wasted no time in doing what they told me.

There was no bathroom in the house. I was the one who had to carry the five gallon bucket that was always full to the top with the family body waste. As I lugged the putrid pail outside, I'd want to vomit from the smell. I had to take it from the house and carry it to my grandparents' outhouse and dump it there.

My body was so dirty and smelled so bad that the bugs would be crawling all over me from head to toe. I would scratch and scratch, but they kept on biting into my skin. It was like I was a piece of dead meat on which they could feast. My hair was dirty and full of head lice. I would scratch and pull my hair, thinking that would make the lice go away. I was happy when the school nurse would check our heads. She would send everyone that had head lice home with a bottle of special shampoo. For a few days my hair would be gloriously clean.

I was an outcast in this family. Patty was Mother's favourite. I was never allowed to touch anything of Patty's. Sometimes visitors would come to our house and give us children little treats. I didn't understand why my treats were always taken away from me and given to Patty. Everything was all about Patty. She was the centre of Mother's world. I really felt like a nobody. Mother would yell at me and say, "Patty had it all until you came along and covered everything

With shit." Mother's words really made me feel dirty. I loved my sister so much, and I wanted Mother to love me as much as she loved Patty. Deep down inside, I knew that would never happen. I was the Black sheep of the family. No matter how hard I tried to fit in, there was no way Mother would ever allow that to happen.

Sandy sits alone on the floor of that cold, dark room. She cries for love,

But who cares? Nobody hears her.

Sandy cuddles herself, trying to smile But all she can do is frown.

No one ever takes time for Sandy. She bears the pain and cries alone ...

And in the darkness of the night, When all are asleep,

Not a sound in the house, But her tiny, stained feet. She walks through the house, Looking for something to eat.

CHAPTER THREE
SURVIVAL

When I was seven, my life, unlike that of most little girls, was not about playing with dolls or dreaming about that fairy-tale wedding I would have when I grew up. My life at that time was about real survival. I never knew what the next day would bring, or even if there was going to be a next day for me. Each night I fell asleep thinking that I might die before morning.

In the summer I loved outside chores. They gave me a sense of freedom, if only for a couple of hours. Creating my own little world, I would venture off into the woods near our home and play out my life the way I wished it could be. I loved the smell of tree leaves and the sound of rippling water. I hated having to leave my utopia. But when my mother's shrill voice broke the barrier of my little world, reality would strike as forcefully as the July heat that engulfed my fragile frame.

Our family's house, in a small community in central Newfoundland, was nothing more than a shack and had no indoor plumbing. I remember it as a cold, dark place with bare wooden floors. Somewhere inside this shack was the little Black room where I was deprived of food or water, not just for a week or two, but for years.

The family subsisted on fish, rabbit, moose, potatoes, home-made bread, powdered milk, tea, coffee, cakes, cookies, and home-made candy. I remember crying for powdered milk. My father made fun of the way I pronounced, "milk power." I called it "milk feta." This persisted until I was eight or nine. Seeing the other children around me with big glasses of milk, I wanted some, but they never gave me any.

In the summer my parents grew a garden that consisted of potatoes, cabbage, carrots, beets, and corn. Mother made homemade jams and pickles. The table was always set to the fullest.

Our house was a very busy one, with visitors coming and going at all times. Mother was never shy with company and always made them feel welcome. That made me happy. When visitors came, there were times that I was allowed out of the dark room and given the freedom to eat with everyone else. What a treat! Night after night people would come and leave with their bellies full. Mother would go all-out to feed them. The visitors were given nothing but the best of whatever food was in the house.

One time Mother's sister was coming home from Toronto for a family visit. That made Mother happy because she didn't get to see her sister very often. Mother spent all week cleaning the house and baking cakes and cookies.

On the day of her sister's visit, Mother cooked up a big family dinner—only the best, as always. When it was time to start, Mother put some food on my plate and told me to eat. But when my aunt saw the small portion of food I had been given, she took my plate back to the big cooking pot, which was sitting on the woodstove. Returning to the table with my plate and noticing that I had no meat as the others did, she took the chicken and salt beef from her plate and put it on mine. I ate everything on my plate. It was great—a real meal! I felt so good, thinking nothing of it because Mother was in a good mood. Having her sister come to visit had made her very happy.

I thought maybe Mother wouldn't beat me that night as I went back to the room with my belly full. I don't remember what time my aunt left, but sometime in the late-night hours I was pulled from a deep sleep and beaten badly for eating the food that my aunt had put on my plate. The next day there were marks on my back and legs again. I was told not to say a word about the beating to anyone. That was my last meal for over a week.

This abuse was ongoing in our home, year after year. The rest of the world outside kept going on as if nothing was different, or as if this small child deserved these punishments each and every day of her life.

I'd often wet and soil my pants, even at school. I did this because I believed I was too dirty to use the bathroom. I was afraid to put my hand up to let the teacher know that I needed to leave the classroom. If my mother found out, I would be in trouble with her too and get beaten for it.

At home and in my little Black room, in an attempt to escape yet another beating, I would urinate on the floor. The urine would just run down through the old wooden boards on the floor. When it came time for a bowel movement, tears would stream down my sunken little face. I knew there was no way out. Again I was forced to do it on the floor, terrified and degraded. I would find some old piece of cloth to cover it up and pray that my mother wouldn't find out about what I had done. The excrement would be all over my hands and the smell would make me sick.

My fondest memories of life in Norris arm are of times spent with my grandparents, my father's parents. I remember my Grandmother Brown so clearly. In my mind's eye I can see her walking down the garden as if it were yesterday. She would be holding up her apron to conceal the big, juicy red apples she would give us. We were so appreciative. As I crunched into the tangy fruit, its juice ran down my chin. With a big smile on my face, I would wipe my mouth with the sleeve of my soiled clothing.

There were days when I'd come home from school with my sister and brother for lunch hour. They'd sit at the table and have a good lunch, while I would stand and eat a small piece of bread. When that piece of bread was eaten, I'd be sent back to school still hungry. On the way there I would go through garbage or pick up things from the ground to eat. Doing this made me feel dirty and ashamed, but I had to eat something to stay alive.

My grandparents lived next door to us. Sometimes they'd watch as I went to the well for water. I'd have to walk through a long woods road with trees on each side. When I'd walked far enough, the trees would hide me. Then I'd stop and wait, knowing one or the other of my grandparents would be coming along with a thick slice of bread smothered with butter and molasses. After I got done eating, l would lie on my belly and have a good drink of cold water from the well.

In the winter, when the snow was knee deep, I still had to get the water. My feet and hands would turn blue from the cold. But I'd still love to bring water because my grandparents' molasses bread would make me forget how cold it was outside.

When Mother would go out for long periods of time, my grandfather would come to visit with my father. Sometimes he'd yell at Father and say, "What in the hell are you doing to Sandra?" Father would say, "It's not me! It's her mother."

One time in particular my father made lunch for himself and Grandfather: bread and tea with fried eggs. Grandfather took his and passed it to me. I looked at him, not sure what to do. It's something I will never forget. It was the first time I had ever gotten a fried egg at home. It made my mouth water just looking at it on the table. Grandfather said, "take it and eat. Never mind your father." My heart was pounding with fear. I knew that if Mother found out about this, I would not get any food for a week, maybe even longer. Suddenly I reached across the table, grabbed the plate, and started to eat as fast as I could. After getting the taste in my mouth it didn't matter to me if Mother found out or not.

Grandfather stayed until I had gone to bed. Later that night, when Mother got home, Father wasted no time telling her what had happened when Grandfather had been at the house that night and how I'd grabbed the plate like a hungry dog and gobbled up the food. Mother started yelling at Father, telling him, "Go and get that

Other Thing ..." Hearing all this, I was wondering why he had to tell her that. At the same time I was trying to tense my body, preparing for what was coming next. Father came to my room, yelling, "Get out here!" Before I got out of the room, he dragged and pulled me out of the room by the hair. He dragged me to where Mother was standing with the belt in her hand.

"I'll give the like of you eating! Who in the hell do you think you are?" She raged. "I'll teach the likes of you to listen!

Eating from someone else's plate when i'm gone!" My father pinned my head between his legs and held my hands. I could hear him telling my mother, "Now give it to her as hard as you can!" Mother brought the belt down on my bare skin, as hard as she could. Father continued to egg her on, saying, "Now come on! Give it to her! That's not enough."

The only time I got an egg after that was when I was in the hospital. My parents didn't take me to the hospital very often, but when they did, I'd be admitted right away. The staff would give me a nice bath and I'd feel so clean. At home I'd sit on the floor of my dark room, picking dirt off my feet, and the small bit of hair on my head was crawling with lice. But in the hospital, when the nurses let me soak in a tub of warm water and put the hospital pajamas on me, I felt so cared for, so normal. And I loved visiting hours because my grandmother and other people would come and visit me, bringing goodie bags filled with candy bars and chips.

One time I was released from the hospital on the day we were to have our christmas party at school. I felt like a princess when my teacher sent me home that day with a prize for being neat and tidy. Usually I was given notes to bring home to my mother because I was always dirty and my hair needed washing. I'd destroy these notes and never let Mother see them because I knew I'd be in trouble and she'd beat me again. I wanted her to be proud of me. But she didn't say anything. It meant so much to me but so little to her. She didn't care about me and wasn't about to give me credit for getting a prize at school.

The kids teased and called me names like Breta Brown's Monster and Half-a-lip Person. I was abused and put down in every way possible. There was just no way out at home

Or at school. It didn't matter where I went; there was always some kind of abuse. My only freedom was in the dark room or during school lessons. But if the teacher had to step out of the classroom for some reason, my classmates would start teasing and bullying me and calling me names.

By the age of seven I had started to fight back. I stole things from those nasty kids who made fun of me. This was my only way to survive. I would tell myself that they were not going to get away with their behaviour anymore and that one day I'd be better than they were. So there I was, into fights just about every day. Some girls got the better of me. But sometimes I would come out the winner, and it made me feel proud just knowing someone was afraid of me enough to run away.

For the first time in my life, I felt like I had some control. At least some kids wouldn't pick on me again. But there was a long list of kids still out there waiting to take their turn to fight with me. Sometimes they'd get together in groups as I stood alone to give it my best shot, but against a group my best just wasn't good enough. They would get me every time. I'd hear them joking as I was getting up from the ground with my clothes covered in dirt. "Go home to Mommy," They'd chant. But I knew that Mommy would be waiting with a belt to beat me. "Don't worry!" They'd laugh. "We'll save our garbage for you."

Just about every day I was going home from school with a bloody nose and new marks to go with the ones that Mother and Father had already put there. I remember trying so hard to get my school work done on time and done right, though I didn't like homework. My reader was a little softcover book, a story about Sally, Dick, Jane, and their dog, Spot. Mother would beat me with my school books and tell me I was stupid and would never amount to anything. She would never help me properly or patiently with my spelling lessons. At school I'd try so hard to get the words right, but I'd get them all mixed up every time. When Mother tested me at home I'd sometimes be able to spell them correctly and I'd feel relieved for a moment, thinking Mother would have one less reason to beat me. But that wasn't good enough for Mother. She would hold the spelling book up high and ask me to spell the words again. This time she would mix them up, and I'd get them wrong every time. She knew I'd learned them in order, and it gave her great joy to tell me to put my hands on the table as she spoke in my face.

"How do you spell 'went'?" She'd ask in a soft voice.

I would spell it "W-H-E-N."

"That's wrong!" She'd thunder. "Spell it again!"

I would just take a guess at it and say, "WHERE."

"No, that's not it!" She would yell. This went on every night for years in our home. Mother would beat me over and over with the books every time I got a word wrong.

For obvious reasons, I didn't like reading or spelling, but I did love mathematics because I always got a high mark. When it came to math tests, I would always do well. It gave me something to feel proud about.

How I survived this period, I'll never know. Those beatings took place every day. I had no playmates or after-school playtime. I knew nothing about those things. They were out of the question.

Sometimes our parents would take us kids for Sunday afternoon rides. My sisters and brother looked forward to these times because they knew they'd be getting a treat.

Father would drive from Norris arm to lewisporte Junction, where he would stop and get ice cream or french fries—for everyone but me. The vinegar they put on their fries smelled delicious. I wanted so much to cry, but if my mother caught me crying, she'd punish me more. I'd put my head down and try not to make a sound or even look up until they were done eating.

I never got to sit on a seat in the car. Our family had too many children to fit in the back seat. Each Sunday, as I sat on the floor of the car, I watched as the other children took turns sitting on the back seat. I'd hear them counting the trees as Father drove along the roads.

Once Mother took us to the store with her and as usual gave all the children an ice cream, leaving me out. The storekeeper, Mr. Whit, seeing what Mother had done, went to the cooler and got an ice cream and gave it to me. Mother smiled and said, in a soft, sweet voice, "Oh, Sandra won't eat that." I wasted no time eating that ice cream as fast as I could. It was a real treat. I knew it would be a long time before that would happen again.

When we got home Mother put the grocery bags on the table and gave me that ice cold look of hers. I knew what was coming next. I tried to tense my body as she started taking off her coat and yelling at the same time. "I'll give the like of you taking ice cream and gobbling it down in you like a hungry dog," She ranted. "Who in the hell do you think you are?" She was moving as fast as she could, trying to find father's belt, but it was nowhere to be seen. Mother was getting all the more upset with me in her frustration at not being able to find the belt.

Finally she grabbed the broom and started to beat me over the head, back, and legs with the handle until it broke. After she stopped beating me, I was told, "Get in that goddamn room and don't show your face out of there anymore today." After that beating, one of my legs hurt so much I walked with a limp for about a week.

Sometimes I would be in the room so long, not allowed to come out, that I'd wet my pants. I would wet them over and over again. It made me very sore. My skin would burn and hurt terribly. I would cry because of the burning sensation. Sometimes my father would grab me and rip my underwear off and beat me badly. "Now, not a sound out of that mouth of yours," He'd warn.

At seven I was always terrified, never knowing what was coming next. Mother's rage seemed to be getting worse as each day passed. I couldn't understand what I was doing wrong to anger her so much. Each night I would tell myself that I'd be a really good girl the next day. That will make Mother happy, I'd think, and she won't beat me ever again because i'm going to work fast to do the things she wants me to do around the house. And she'll feed me just like she does the other children. That will make me happy, and I won't have to look for food on the ground to eat because i'm so hungry all the time.

Over and over I wondered how God could let this happen. I couldn't understand how christian parents could have such hate in their hearts toward their own little child. I would wonder, as each day slipped away, what was wrong with me. Weeks and months turned into long years. Time seemed to have no end.

Looking in the window of an old house, What do I see? A little girl, covered with dirt, Nothing on her cold feet. She looks as if she hasn't Eaten in weeks.

I cry, "God, please help! We must make this little girl strong, And get her back on her feet." As I reach out, The tears fall. I turn as White as a sheep.

I cry again, "God, she's not alive." God says, "Fear not, for the child is asleep."

With that, She takes my hand and speaks. "My name is Sandra. Please find me something to eat."

CHAPTER FOUR

MY BIRTHDAY CAKES

I was born on my uncle's birthday. Every year my aunt would make a big birthday cake for my uncle. Then, after they had their family dinner and the cutting of the cake, there was always lots left over. She would make the cake so big that it had to be baked in a turkey roasting pan. She did this so that she could bring the other half to our house as a birthday gift for me.

Mother would tell me to put it away for later. After my aunt and uncle left our house, Mother would make sure everyone had a piece of my birthday cake—everyone, that is, but me. I remember this happening every year until I was about fourteen years old. My wish each year was to have a piece of that cake. My birthday cake. That wish never came true. All I got was just to look at the beautiful molasses fruit cake, covered with white frosting with pretty blue and yellow flowers and green leaves. I sure did appreciate what my sweet aunt did for me. I will never forget the sight of those beautiful cakes she made year after year to make my birthday special.

As a child growing up, I thought: Why don't they like me? Why are they so ashamed of me? I remember thinking: What do I look like? What is wrong with me? I was a little short girl and didn't see my face in a mirror until the year I turned eleven.

There were times when they'd let me stand at the dinner table, but I could never sit down with the other children or eat like them. I was to stand, eat my slice of bread, and then get away from the table, as the rest of the family sat and enjoyed their meal together. When Mother allowed me at the table, there was always a stick of wood on the table where she sat. Often she would look at me and say, "If you do it again, you'll get this." Holding the stick in her hand, she'd yell at me over and over, "You're going to get this." But I didn't know what I was doing wrong, and Mother wouldn't tell me.

I would cautiously take a big bite from my bread. Then Mother would yell at me again. I would think that maybe I was eating too fast. So I'd take little bites, like a mouse nibbling cheese in a trap. That wouldn't work either. Mother would just yell over and over, "Get away from the table!" Dropping my bread in fright, I would try to get into the dark room as fast as I could, before the stick of wood that Mother was holding in her hand hit me. Still to this day I don't know what it was that Mother didn't like about me.

I would be hungry, sick, very cold, and afraid all the time. I lived like a hungry dog. Outside my little room, my eyes would always be wide open, searching for food everywhere. I foraged for anything I could get my hands on while I was fetching wood, carrying well water, or walking to and from school.

Time after time I'd say to myself, if I ever live to get out of here, I'll eat everything I can get my hands on. No one will ever stop me or tell me to get in that room ever again.

I remember sitting there on the cold floor, awake, listening to every creak. The nights were so cold, and the sound of rats terrified me as they scratched in the walls. As I hugged myself to keep warm, I kept dreaming about when I'd grow up and have children of my own, and how I would let them eat all they wanted and keep them clean and warm. When it was time for them to go to school, other children would never make fun of them like my schoolmates did every day. I'd have a hot meal waiting for them when they got home, and we'd sit at the table together, as a family. No one would be left out. My children would never be cold or hungry.

I would wonder whether I'd ever live to see that dream come true. Many nights I would drift off to sleep holding onto those thoughts. On the coldest night in the winter, those dreams were all I had to keep me warm. I would think about when my children's birthdays would come each year, and how special I would want them to feel on the day of their birth. I'd imagine how my children would come home from school with big smiles on their faces, knowing that somewhere in the house; their mother had a beautiful cake waiting to be cut. I'd think about how important it would be that the first piece of cake went to the birthday person.

The days were so long and the nights so cold. The winds made their mournful sounds. It seemed like the nightmare would never end.

My grandparents, my father's parents who lived next door, were so good to me and helped me as much as they could. Grandfather would put us on the horse and sleigh and give us rides—sometimes to school or just for fun. Every time he went to the store for food, he always got a bag of candy for us. He would give each of us the same share. No one got more than the others.

Mother didn't like that he gave me candy in front of her, and that he would stay until she went out somewhere for the evening. On her way out the door, she would give me that cold look of hers. I knew what was coming later. It didn't matter to her if I was sleeping when she came back. She wasn't about to forget or let me have a good night's sleep. Within minutes of her return home, the yelling started. It was always between two and three o'clock in the morning. The time of night didn't matter to Mother. She'd beat me for eating that candy. I'd be thinking to myself that the other children had eaten the candy and didn't get beaten for it. What was so wrong with me? Why was I not allowed to have candy, when the other children were?

My Grandfather Brown was at our house a lot because sometimes Father was gone away all week for work and didn't come home until Friday night. Grandfather—or Pop, as we called him—would come to make sure there was enough wood to keep the house warm. One day Mother started yelling and screaming at me, and fearing for my life, I called for help. Joey and Patty were yelling, "Mom, stop! You're going to kill Sandra!" My brother yelled to my sister to go and get Pop. Soon Pop was on his way down to our house to stop Mother, but she wouldn't let him in. She knew he was at the door to stop the beating. Hearing him, Mother became even more furious as she continued beating me. But Pop was not about to give up. He knew he had to act very fast. He quietly left our house, ran to his shed, got his axe, and chopped his way through the door. He then stopped Mother from beating me.

When Father returned home from work on the weekend, Mother told him that Grandfather had forced his way into the house. I never saw Father more enraged in my life. You could hear him for miles, raging at Grandfather: "Get down here, you! Goddamn son of a bitch! I'll chop the two fucking legs right off at your hips."

Lucky for Grandfather, one of the neighbours called the police in lewisporte. That was the nearest police station to where we lived at the time. Two police officers came to our house to talk about what had happened. They asked my parents if they wanted to lay charges. Mother said no, but she asked if there was anything else that could be done to keep Mr. Brown away from the house. One of the officers told them he could put a peace bond on Grandfather. That would stop him from coming anywhere near our family or our house.

Father said, "Yes, go ahead and do that."

The officers then went to Grandfather's house and ordered him to stay away from us. Once again Mother had succeeded in getting rid of the one person who had reached out to help and protect me. Grandfather was very upset. He didn't understand what was going on. All he had ever done for the family was to give us a helping hand when we needed it.

After that day we saw Grandfather only when we were going or coming from the water well. We'd meet him carrying his aluminum water buckets. Sometimes on our way to school we kids would see him with his horse and sleigh, going to the store to get food. We missed him so much, along with the things he did for us without Mother knowing. We'd pass him with our heads down, feeling terrible for him. We'd walk slowly and not make eye contact with him, waiting until he was out of sight to look up.

Winter turned into spring, spring into summer, and summer into fall. Finally Mother gave in and asked Father to go and talk to Grandfather and ask if he wanted to come for a cup of tea. We were all so happy to have Grandfather back again. It was just like old times. Night after night Mother would be gone. We'd sit and listen to Grandfather's stories. Father, his brother Zack, and Pops would swap stories about boats, horses, and who was the fastest skater in Norris Arm. They'd go on for hours each night, as we sat around the old woodstove, listening.

Many nights I would wish for time to stand still. I was out of the cold, dark room, sitting with the other children. On those precious nights I felt like I was a part of the family. But that special feeling lasted only until my grandfather and uncle Zack left each night, shortly before Mother's return home. One of the children would warn, "Mom's coming up the driveway!"

That's when Father would say to me, "Now get in the goddamn room as fast as you can go and don't come out!" I would be so afraid, not understanding why Father would turn on me so quickly. It seemed like he loved me, and then, all of a sudden, he was angry with me.

With the passage of years I thought I finally understood why. He didn't want Mother to know that he had let me out of the room and fed me while she was gone. It was his way of protecting me from Mother and her outrage. Now, though, I have to wonder if he was really out to help me or if he was just protecting himself from her anger. Father was so afraid of what Mother might do to him. He was terrified that she might leave him, as she had so often threatened.

Night after night Mother would come home and fight with Father over some crazy thing. All the children would be awakened by Mother's yelling. Father would never fight back. That would make Mother even more enraged. On those nights the household would be crazy—the children crying, Mother throwing things around the house. Along with all the other noises, I could hear the creaks every time Mother stomped across the wooden floor. With every creak my body would tense with fear that Mother was on her way to drag me out of my dark room for another beating. My Father wouldn't fight back, so she would take her fury out on me. I was the one who got punished for whatever went wrong in her life, no matter what the problem was. Mother didn't care or stop to think that I'd already had the crap kicked out of me earlier that day. The more father said, "That's enough!" The harder she'd hit me. Over and over. No one could stop her.

At the time I wished someone would tell me what I was doing wrong so I could make it all turn out right next time. It seemed that the other children could do no wrong. No matter how hard I tried to do things right, my best just wasn't good enough to please Mother. There was just no way she was ever going to like me or accept me as one of her children. I was just the Other Thing that belonged in the dark room and got food only when Mother felt like feeding me.

Most of the time I was forgotten. I was left in that cold room for days at a time without food or water. No one checked to see if I was even alive. Sometimes the voices outside my room became so low that I couldn't hear them anymore. My body would get so weak sitting on the floor that I couldn't sit up, and I'd feel myself falling to the side. My eyes would close, but then I'd fight to keep them open because I didn't want to die that way. I'd comfort myself with the idea that someone would come to get me out of there before I died.

Sometimes I would open my eyes and see shadows that looked like people. I could hear people talking to me, but they sounded far away from where I was lying on the floor. I couldn't pick out what they were trying to say or what they wanted me to do. I tried to talk and tell them that I was sick and couldn't move my body, but I was too weak to speak.

Then Mother's giant shadow would loom over me. She'd stare at me as if I were just a piece of dirt on the floor. Father would pick up my tiny body and feed me some food. Patty would bring something to cover my cold body. Within minutes I'd start to feel better. The shadows I'd seen would become real people. Their voices would grow much louder than before. I would then realize that I'd been drifting in and out of consciousness. When this happened, I would be nursed back to health with bread and water. No one considered taking me to the hospital. I was malnourished, dehydrated, sick from the cold, and beaten nearly to death.

As I sit and write my story, I realize that all it would have taken to get help was for someone to make one little phone call to the police. But no one cared enough to do that. I sit here now in my warm house with more food than I could ever want. I see the Black telephone in my head, the one the family used all those years ago. They could reach the outside world for anything they wanted, from buying a horse to seeing a doctor. But no one—not my father, my grandfather, or my grandmother—thought to make that one call.

An identical Black telephone hung on my Grandfather Brown's wall beside the window for all those years. I remember looking up at that phone every time I went to his house. I was amazed that, just by dialing a few numbers, you could talk to anyone. That phone was just a few steps from where we lived. Father could have gone there anytime to use it, but he never did.

I went to school every day thinking that there was something wrong with me because no one wanted me around. I couldn't see my own face because I was too short to see myself in the bathroom mirror at school as the other girls did. They'd look in the mirror to comb their shiny clean hair. I'd go into the bathroom stalls and look at myself in the chrome bathroom tissue holders. I remember seeing a funny square face. By then I was truly convinced that I was a short, ugly, stupid little girl. I knew that I had no place in a world with other children or my family. Through my eyes all I saw was an ugly, unwanted girl. I'd tell myself hopefully that when I grew up, I'd be pretty. Everybody would like me. I'd have clean hair and pretty dresses to wear.

I remember wanting a pretty ring on my finger. Sometimes I would twist some old piece of wire together and put it on my finger as a ring. I'd picture it as a beautiful diamond. But that was just another of my childhood fantasies. I was fifteen years old when I got my first ring. It was gold with two white fake pearls. The boy who gave me this ring really liked me a lot and asked me to be his girlfriend. I loved that ring so much. I kept touching it and picking at the pearls. Soon all the white came off them. But I still kept showing it off to all my friends. I would always take it off before getting home so Mother wouldn't see it on my finger. I knew she'd get mad and make me throw it away.

My second ring was an eighteenth birthday gift from my sister Patty. It was the most beautiful ring I'd ever seen. It made me so happy. I felt so rich wearing my first real gold ring with my birthstone mounted in a delicate setting.

Who will care for a little girl With messy hair, torn dress, no socks, bruised face? She cries and cries because she's had nothing to eat ... So badly bruised you can barely see her faint cheeks.

Her eyes are sunken because she can't sleep. She's so afraid of the light because she's Buried so dark in the deep ...

Who will take her hand, Walk her down the street? This little girl may even stop and Pick things off the street to eat. Please watch your neighbours' garbage Because this little girl may find it. Tastes so sweet!

Who will help this little girl? I will Because I am This little girl Who walked the streets, Looking for something to eat.

Justice Prevails

CHAPTER FIVE

MY FATHER'S FAMILY

My father was the youngest of five children. He had two brothers and two sisters. Grandmother and Grandfather made a family of seven. Father was born on april 15, 1933. He grew up in the little town of Norris arm North. That was back when times were hard and most people didn't have much to live on. Father went to school for a very short time, leaving at grade two and never returning.

As a young man he went to work to help support his family. He did the only thing he ever knew how to do: working with wood. Father got great joy out of making things from old wood pieces. Among the things he made were wooden whistles. He'd also make spinning tops out of the old wooden spools that thread came on back in those years. He went to work at the town sawmill as a manual labourer. Father was never shy about doing a hard day's work. If there was a way to make money, he was there.

The family home was very small and had no running water or indoor bathroom. Getting water from the well and chopping firewood was all work done by hand. Father and his brothers worked hard all day and long hours after dark. After the firewood was cut, in the fall of the year when the ground got hard, they would work with the horse and sleigh. Even the dogs were used to haul the wood to keep them warm in the winter months.

Grandmother worked hard making quilts for the same purpose. She did all the cooking to feed the family. Many nights she was out giving a helping hand to get the winter wood. Grandmother was a very strong-willed, powerful woman. If she set her mind to do something, there was no talking her out of it. She was a straight shooter who would take on anyone. She worked like a real lady in the house and did what she had to do for the family. If she was needed outside, she worked hard with her boys and kept right up with them.

Grandmother and Grandfather Brown came from Joe Batt's Arm. I don't know if they ever returned for a visit after moving away, but I do remember how much Grandfather wanted to go back and have a good old chat with friends that he grew up with. Father and his two brothers and one sister stayed in Newfoundland and lived and raised their families there. These siblings kept in touch over the years.

One sister went away to live in Toronto at a very young age and never came back to visit the family. No one ever heard from her until the summer of 1975, when Father went to Toronto for a visit. Father would travel from Norris Arm to Peterview in his motorboat to visit his brother Zack and his family. While visiting at his brother's house one night, Father met and fell in love with Mother. He married her in the 1950s. They lived with his parents for a while until they got a little place of their own. With help from his brothers and the men from the town, they built a little house in Norris arm North.

Mother and Grandmother didn't get along well. They were always having words over something. Father had been blindsided by his love for Mother. This made things rough for him because he loved his mother so much, it hurt him to take sides. This was just the start of a long battle between the love he had for his birth family and what he felt for my mother. In Father's eyes Mother could do no wrong. But Grandmother was not about to let Mother run the family that she had worked so hard for. Grandmother loved us children like we were her own. Mother knew it would be a losing battle when it came to fighting with Grandmother, so she would get very upset and take it out on Father. There were times when Father didn't talk to his parents and siblings because of this. Somehow he had to keep peace with Mother, and if that meant staying away from his family then so be it.

Times were getting harder for our own family each year with the birth of new babies to feed. That meant longer hours for Father at work. But he never once gave up and never took time off. Even when he was sick, he pushed through it all to make ends meet. He left Mother in control of all the money. Through all the fighting and words being said, Father never fell out with his own family, even though at times it would be months before any contact was made. The family knew Mother was behind it all. Unlike Father, the rest of the family saw Mother for what she really was. So year after year they would let Mother's words go in one ear and out the other, if that's what it took to keep the peace and stay close to Father.

November 25, 1966, would be Grandmother Brown's last day to walk on her own. This was one of the saddest days of my life. I'll never forget how helpless I felt when Joey and I found her lying on the cold ground. The snow was lightly falling that afternoon at about three-thirty. I can see Grandmother as if it was yesterday, lying there so helpless, trying to call for help. Her lips were moving but her words were not coming through.

That day had started out like most school days. We'd come home for lunch. Mother and the other children had sat down to eat. I was told to go outside and bring wood into the house because it was going to be stormy that night. My brother and sister went back to school. I was to stay home to finish bringing in the wood and get the house cleaned. While I was chopping the wood that afternoon, I watched Grandmother Brown walking toward the woods with water pots in her hands. All she was wearing over her cotton dress was a little green sweater. I didn't think too much of it and went back to my work.

Later that evening Joey came home from school and wanted some molasses on his bread. We didn't have any in the house, so Mother told him to go borrow some from Grandmother. Joey came back from Grandmother's house and told Mother that Grandmother wasn't home.

Knowing that Grandmother was never far from home, Mother said, "are you sure? She must be there somewhere. Go check the shed or the horse barn." When Joey came back, he reported that he couldn't find Grandmother. She was nowhere to be found.

I said, "Mother, when I was getting wood earlier today, I saw Grandmother go to the well for water."

Mother yelled at me, "Did you see her come back from the woods?"

In a low voice I mumbled no.

Mother then sent Joey and me to look for her and to bring water at the same time. With our water buckets we set off slowly toward the well. As we walked we looked on both sides. All we saw were the tall trees. It was now getting a little dark. Joey started to cry. I took him by the hand and said, "It's okay, Joey. The sounds are just birds singing in the trees."

About halfway to the well we noticed Grandmother lying on the ground with her feet in a puddle of ice water. She looked very much like she was dead. Joey dropped his buckets and began to scream, "She's dead! She's dead! Nan is on the ground dead!" He ran away, jumping over the fence. I'll never forget that day as long as I live. By the time I'd gotten back to the house, Mother was coming toward me yelling out the words, "Go! Get help!"

With the help of neighbours Mother got Grandmother back to the house. She called Grandfather, who was at the store, and he came home right away. With Mother he hurried off again to the hospital with Grandmother.

Later we learned that Grandmother wasn't dead but had suffered a stroke and had been lying on the cold ground for about four hours in just a sweater over her thin dress. The doctor said that she was paralyzed and would never walk or talk again. So from that day forward until the time of her death, Grandmother lived like a baby. She had to be fed by someone in her green reclining chair. That's how she lived out the rest of her life. She had to be picked up and carried to bed at night. When morning came, Grandfather would carry her from her bed back to the green chair. I remember many times when she got very sick and had to be taken back to the hospital.

One time in winter it was stormy outside, and the wind was blowing the snow so hard you couldn't even see the house next door. Everything was just white from the blowing snow. Father said, "We've got to get her to the doctor somehow tonight because she won't live until morning." Leaving the house, he looked at Grandfather. Father said, "Get back on the phone and keep calling until you find someone that will drive us to the hospital. I'll get the sleigh ready," He said. "We have to get her down to the road." Mother hurried to get blankets to put on the sleigh to keep Grandmother warm because it was a long way from the house to the road.

Again we were all so worried. We didn't want Grandmother to die. But all we could do was stand around and watch as Father and Grandfather carried her outside and put her on the sleigh. Father was at the front, pulling, and Grandfather was at the back to push the sleigh though the snowy drifts to the car that was waiting at the road.

Grandmother's health had worsened because there was no home care back in those days. Grandfather did the best he could to care for her, and the rest of the family took their turn to give Grandfather and Mother a rest.

The day we found Grandmother on the ground, I was seven years old. Joey was five. We were both very upset and in shock about finding our Grandmother like this. But still I was ordered to go back to the well every day for water. In my mind every day I'd still see my Grandmother lying there on the ground, looking at me with that blank stare so much like she was dead. It was sad to see our Grandmother this way, knowing that she would not be able to walk on her own or talk ever again. She was so sick all the time, but there wasn't anything we could do to help her feel better.

Father and Grandfather would do most of the lifting and Mother would do the cleaning and combing her hair.

Grandmother didn't like for Mother to touch her at all. Every time Mother went to comb her hair, Grandmother would look at Mother and make a funny noise. Mother now had control over Grandmother, and Mother let her know it. Every time she combed Grandmother's hair, she would pull it really hard.

Grandmother meant so much to us children. She had a little house with one bedroom, a small kitchen, and a room where they kept food and water. There was a wooden table off to the side wall. There wasn't even room enough to pull it out to eat. At the back wall were four chairs in a row. That's where visitors would sit. There was a little shelf on the side wall where Grandmother kept her dishes.

Outside, in front of the house, were three big apple trees and a damson plum tree. Grandmother had planted them when my father and his brothers and sisters were just little children. The trees were old but the apples and damsons were so good. We always had food to eat at my Grandmother's house when we went to visit. We kids sure did miss Grandmother's apple pies and baked beans. I loved the way she made her beans. She would always bake them with lots of salt pork and onions. To this day, any time I make baked beans, I do them the way Grandmother did hers. The pork buns she made were also delicious. I've made them but they never once turned out as good as Grandmother's.

Father and his brothers would tell stories about how strong she was. We would sit there and listen to them like they were reading it all from a book. As little children we learned a lot from the stories they told. What else did we have? There was no tv back in those days. There was just school and lots of hard work. Some children were lucky enough to have colouring books and crayons.

Grandmother Brown died in the early 1970s. But her memory will live in my heart forever. In so many ways all the girls in the Brown family are so much like her. We are all strong when it comes to getting through hard times. When we put our minds to doing something, there's no stopping us.

Father was a hard worker and never asked for much. He loved to spend time with his brothers. I remember Father and his brother, uncle Zack, being together a lot over the years. Just about every night after dinner, you could look out the window and see uncle Zack and his wife, aunt lil, coming for a visit. I loved it when they came to our house because I knew their visits would be four to five hours each night, and I wouldn't get beaten until they'd gone home.

Father was a smart man in so many ways. He could take an old piece of pine wood and make a beautiful boat, paint it up, and you would think it came from a store. Many times, men would call on him to come and take a look at an old boat that had been lying up on the beach somewhere, full of holes and not good for anything. Father would bring that old thing home and make it look like new again. He didn't have power tools to work with, just a few hand tools and a picture in his head.

He loved to sing. Mother would yell at him to shut up. Given the man he was, he never once spoke back. He would just walk outside and keep busy until she went out visiting somewhere. Then he would come back inside and start singing. Sometimes he would change the words and add something funny to the song. I think he laughed at himself more than we would laugh at what he was singing. I would say, "Dad, that's not the right words to that song!"

He would just look at me with that big smile of his and say, "Never you mind now, my dear. That's a lot better than the words in the song to begin with."

One of his favourite songs was "two little Orphans," And another was "take This Message to My Mother." He would sing a lot of old silly things, but those two are the songs I remember him singing.

Father was silly in other ways too and liked to make funny faces to make us laugh at him. He learned more from his children than we did from him. He could sharpen skates better than anyone in town. All the kids in town would bring their skates to our house for Father to sharpen. They'd give him a dollar for it. Father would be very proud. He'd pass the money over to Mother, just as he did with every other dollar he worked for over the years.

Father was not a man to be a drinker or get drunk. He never saw the inside of a beer store. Anytime he would go to a family wedding or some special party, he would go up to the bar and get a beer and that would do him all night long. I remember many times asking him if he would like to have a beer, but he would say, "No, my dear. I got no time for that drinking and making a fool of myself."

One time the family held a birthday party for him. Everyone was having a good time, dancing and doing silly things. But Father was just sitting there, watching the people on the dance floor. I said, "Dad, go and have a dance." I knew he was upset because Mother was off dancing with all the men in the bar but wouldn't dance with him. My best friend was with us at the party that night. With a smile she said, "come on, Mr. Brown. Let's go dance. This is your night." He was happy about that. Then all the ladies took a turn dancing with him. That was the highlight of his night. Everyone loved Father. But like me, they couldn't understand why he always let Mother have control.

Over the years many people have asked me how I could love my parents. I don't know why and can't understand it myself. I love them as parents. But at the same time I hate them for what they did to me as a child.

I know in my heart Father loved me and was very proud of the lady I turned out to be in life. What I don't understand is why he took part in beating me. Being the strong man that he was, he usually stood up for everything that he felt was right. Yet not once did he stand up to protect me from Mother.

So many times I looked into his eyes as a beating went on, silently begging him to have mercy on me and make the hurt stop. But my unspoken cries for help were never heeded. I remember, many times during the beatings, hearing my father's voice saying to me, "You won't do it again, will you? You're going to listen to your mother." "Yes, Dad," I'd assure him. "I'll listen. I'll be good for Mom." Even these words didn't stop them. They went on and on with the beatings for what seemed like hours at a time. Mother would use every bit of strength she had in her body before she would stop. I would cry over and over, "Dad! I didn't do it!" When accused, I'd protest, "I didn't see it! I don't know what happened to it. It wasn't me."

I would think: Why can't you hear me, Dad? Why don't you listen to my screaming for help or feel my pain? You're so strong and smart. I know you love me like you love the other children in the house. Why are you letting this happen to me? I'm not doing anything wrong. I'm crying because it hurts so much and i'm so hungry. I need food, Daddy. Just a piece of bread and some water. Food will take some of the pain away. Can't you understand that?

You were my dad. A dad is supposed to know and feel those things about his little girl. What was wrong with you? Why didn't you say no to Mother? Couldn't you see? Didn't you know I'd had enough? Didn't you care? How could you have been so unfeeling? Why didn't you tell Mother, "I will no longer take part in what you're doing to Sandra."

Who was this man I called Father? Why was it that I felt his pain but not one time over the years did he feel mine? My father died on February 20, 2010, just days before my fifty-first birthday. Even though he now resides in an unknown world, I lie awake at night and wonder why he didn't stop the beatings and why he didn't hear my cries.

In truth, I don't understand where this love I feel for my father comes from. If I had the power within me to reach out and bring him back to my world, I would do it in a heartbeat, and I would show him what he did to his little girl. I'd wrap my arms around him and say, "It's okay, Daddy. I'm a big girl now. I can handle whatever the world dishes out for me, thanks to all those beatings, sleepless nights, and going hungry." I'm now strong enough to reach inside myself and free the little girl that's been hurting for all those years and tell her about how weak the man she called Daddy really was.

So, as my father rests somewhere high on a hilltop or low in a dark valley without light, my life goes on. I no longer fear him hurting me in the night.

Have you ever wondered What it would be like to run and play with children after school?

Or maybe just to watch them play with their toys as Mommy puts dinner on the table, To watch them put their tiny hands into the cookie jar.

Have you ever wondered How nice it would be To sit with your brothers and sisters Just to watch TV?

I fantasized about being Daddy's little girl, Having him bounce me On his knee As the sun goes down.

Have you heard Mommy saying, "Come here, darling. I'm proud of you. When you grow up, You'll have a family of your own. Then you can tell them stories Of all the happy times we shared."

But because of parents With no love in their hearts, All those things are denied to you.

CHAPTER SIX

WHY WAS MY PAIN NOT IMPORTANT?

This has to be one of the more disgusting sides of my story. But nevertheless it's part of my life. At the age of seven, day and night I had an unbearable pain in my mouth. Not knowing at the time what it was, I didn't dare tell Mother. I was terrified of what she would do to me.

So off I went to school. But the pain continued to get worse, and I couldn't stop myself from crying. My teacher noticed my tears and asked me what was wrong. I told her my tooth was hurting me. All the kids in class started laughing and making fun of me because I couldn't understand why the teacher wasn't seeing the pain inside my mouth. At that age I didn't understand that pain was something you felt but did not see.

My teacher took me aside and explained to me that the pain I was having was from a toothache. She decided to send me home. Home was the last place I wanted to go. I dried my eyes and hoped to hear the teacher say, "come back, Sandra. I'll get you something for your pain." But the response didn't come, so I walked slowly toward the classroom door.

I knew Mother would be outraged with me for coming home. Things were not going to be good for me that evening. So I took my time walking home. I looked at the homes along the roadside and wished that I could live in one of them. They looked so pretty. Some of them had beautiful flowers of all colours. Everything around those yards looked so clean. The smell of food cooking as I walked past each house was so tantalizing. I pictured myself sitting at the table in each house and being able to eat from a plate and drink tea from a cup without being afraid of getting hit with a stick of wood.

As I got to our house, all the beautiful thoughts vanished from my head. I prepared myself for what was coming. When I walked in the door, Mother said, "What in the hell is wrong with you?" Before I had a chance to answer her, she lifted her hand and hit me on the side of the face. "I'll give the likes of you coming home from school!" She shouted. I just stood there stunned. I couldn't believe a mother could be so cruel, knowing I was in so much pain.

I was a seven-year-old child. I didn't understand at the time that there was an abscess in my gum. I only knew there was a terrible sick taste in my mouth and a swelling that had a bad-smelling liquid draining from it. That made me sick because I was swallowing most of it, knowing that if Mother saw me spitting, she would beat me.

The terrible pain was all up the side of my face and around my right ear. It went on for over a week before it suddenly stopped. I now understand that the abscess must have broken. Mother never once took the time to check on me or give me anything to help the pain go away.

It wasn't long after this that Patty came home crying with a toothache. Right away Mother was in a big hurry to give her something for the pain. Throughout the night the pain got worse. Both Mother and Father were up most of the night, trying things to relieve the pain, so everyone could get some sleep. In the morning they took Patty to see a doctor and maybe have the tooth taken out.

I watched as my parents carried Patty off to see the doctor in lewisporte. He removed the tooth, and within a few hours they were home again. I felt so bad for Patty. I knew how painful it was to have a toothache like that. But my toothache went on for a week and nothing was done until it went away on its own.

Mother always babied Patty when she was sick, making sure she had all the right foods such as soups, Jell-O, and pudding to eat and milk and juices to drink until she was feeling better. I'd always wondered over the years what the difference was between my sister's pain and mine. I was not allowed to cry or talk about my pain to anyone. I could hear my sister crying many times about how much her pain hurt.

I remember sitting on the floor of that cold dark room, thinking to myself as I listened to my sister crying. What makes her pain so special? Not one time did Mother or Father yell at her or tell her to shut up and stop that crying. When they noticed me crying at any time over pain, they would yell and tell me, "Shut that goddamn mouth of yours or I'll give you something to cry about."

So I bore my pains in silence as days slipped into nights and nights into weeks. I was all alone. I had no help, no one to care about me. All I had were a few small dreams to keep me going. I repeated over and over to myself, like a mantra: if I ever live to get out of here, they will never hurt me again.

That was my silent cry, my dream, my ray of hope. By the time I was seven, the beatings and neglect were an everyday thing. My body became so numb that most of the time I didn't feel the beatings. But I would feel the blood dripping down my legs, and my body would twitch as Mother came down on me, landing blow after blow with every ounce of power she had, showing no mercy.

I remember trying to cover a burning spot with my hands so she wouldn't hit me in the same area again. Mother would yell, "Get your hands out of there!" She couldn't see that my skin was being burned by being hit so many times with the belt in the same spot. My injuries would form big scabs on my back and legs. Every time I took off my dress and tights, my clothes would be stuck to the scabs. As I pulled my things off, the scabs would come off as well and the open sores would bleed.

One year all three of us kids got the measles at the same time. Patty, Joey, and I were all home from school because our bodies were just covered with spots. As always, I was left alone to wait until the rash went away on its own. Patty and Joey got special cream to rub on their bodies to stop the itching so they wouldn't scratch themselves and get infected. Mother called to place an order for milk and then went shopping for special food for them to eat. Once again I was in my little room as they got special attention until their infections were gone. I sat there and wondered: What is the difference between their measles and mine? Why am I not getting milk and special foods to feel better? Why am I not being given any cream to stop my itching?

I still had to go outside to bring the wood and water into the house. Father was away working. I wasn't even allowed to rest or given time to get better like the other kids. I was seven years old, alone, hungry, and cold, sitting on the floor in the dark room, with my body covered in measles.

I tried hard not to think about the pain by saying over and over to myself: it doesn't hurt; I don't feel the pain; it's all in my head. I'd fall asleep hoping that in the morning things would be better. I hoped against hope that Mother would feel bad and treat me the same as the other children.

I was happy when it came time to go back to school. I carried scars for a long time after that because I'd scratched myself so much that the rash had gotten infected. But even with my illness behind me, every morning I'd still wake up on that hard floor.

Things were the same, day after day. Some mornings I'd be lucky and get a slice of bread with butter for breakfast. My brother and sister would be given a bowl of hot cereal and a glass of milk or juice. They'd set off for school every day carrying Mother's home-made treats, while on many days I'd go to school with a gnawing hunger in the pit of my stomach. I would dream of having just enough food to take the hunger pangs away. My eyes were always alert, searching for food. It didn't matter to me whether it came off the ground or someone's table. To a starving child, any food tastes good.

Sometimes, when no one was looking, I would take food from the dog's dish. I'd cram it into my mouth as fast as I could, shivering with the fear of getting caught. There was no time to look around to see if anyone saw me. I had to get something into my stomach to satisfy my hunger. If it kept the family dog alive, then it would keep me alive as well. When I was caught, I was sent to bed without supper.

I remember vividly an old green and white house along the roadside. Many days I'd come home for lunch hour but was sent back to school again still very hungry. On my way back to school I'd pass this house. Sometimes I'd look and there, sitting on the bank by this house, I'd find the remains of a raisin pie. To me this was a banquet. I'd pick that pie up, brush any dirt from it, and eat it as fast as I could. It seemed like a miracle. Looking back today, I believe that it wasn't just an accident. That pie was waiting for me on my way to school. Someone knew and understood my pain, and this was their way of reaching out to help.

I thank God for good people with kind hearts willing to help a child they didn't even know. I remember this man who would come to visit at our house once in a while. He would always talk to me nicely. He'd touch my head and kiss me on the face. He was always well-dressed and had beautiful Black hair combed back with the wet look. Mother was always so happy when he came to our house. She would dress up to look pretty, with her hair nicely done and a little makeup on her face. I don't recall who this man was, but one time he came with a six-pack of drinks and gave us kids one each. We were all at the table that night, just after dark. I remember my bottle of drink was orange. The man took the top off and gave it to me. I remember looking at it for the longest time, not knowing what to do, wondering if I could take a drink or not. But Mother was so happy that night that I put the bottle of pop to my mouth and took a few sips.

Just as I was feeling safe and free to enjoy my drink, Mother came from behind me. As I got the bottle to my mouth again and was about to take a drink, Mother elbowed me in the back of the head. The blow pushed my face forward into the pop bottle. It broke one of my front teeth and cut my mouth enough to make it bleed. That was her way of telling me not to drink the pop and I would get what was coming to me later that night. There I was again, sitting in pain, watching my brother and sisters drink and enjoy their big bottles of pop.

The nice man came over to where I was sitting. He was very concerned that my mouth was bleeding. He hadn't seen Mother hit me and didn't know why I was bleeding. Mother was sweet to him and said, "Oh, she must have hit her mouth with the bottle when she was trying to take a drink." Mother looked at me and said, "Now put that pop away for later and go clean the blood off your chin." That's the first and last time I got a bottle of pop as a child.

*

I'm scared. My body is so cold. My stomach hurts with hunger. I close my eyes and pray:

"God, please let Mother see and feel my pain. Let her know how cold my body is. I'll be a good girl and do everything she asks of me.

"I'm hungry and it hurts. I've been sick now for a long time, but Mother can't see that. I can't cry because she'll beat me again. But God, I am just a little girl and don't know why she doesn't love me the way she loves my brother and sisters. Why doesn't she just tell me what i'm doing wrong, so I won't do it again?

"I know it's wrong to steal food in the night, God, but I must stay alive, and it's just a piece of bread. I'm so cold. God, please help me keep warm through the night.

"God bless Mommy and Daddy. God bless my sister Patty. God bless my brother Joey. God bless my sister ellie. God bless my sister Massy. God bless my baby sister christine.

"If I die before I wake, please, God, my soul is yours to take.

"amen."

*

When I would finish my prayer, I would hold myself tight to keep warm through the night and try not to make a sound. I listened and waited for the family to be asleep, so I could tiptoe out of the dark room and find something to eat. I would eat leftover bread crusts and any other crumbs that I could find left on the plates from what the kids didn't eat because it was burnt. It was so cold and dark, the night wind sounded so scary, and I was terrified of getting caught. I couldn't make any fast moves because Mother would hear me. I would reach my hands up on the table to feel around for any bit of food, telling myself to be strong. Then like a ghost I'd make my way back into the cold, dark room, with luck not getting caught and beaten again. Just a small piece of bread was what I looked forward to every night to stop the pain and keep me alive for a little longer.

My dream was to make it out of that room and that house and away from that woman called Mother—and make it out alive. My mouth watered at the sight of any food. I remember the smell of Mother's chicken soup. There were a few times when Mother would order me to stand at the table as they all sat down to eat, and she would put a small bowl of soup and a spoon in front of me. I'd look at my sisters and watch how they used their spoons. I didn't know how to hold one properly. Every time I scooped the spoon into my soup, Mother would yell at me, "That's not the way you hold a spoon!" I was so afraid of getting hit with the stick that was sitting on the table beside Mother. Terrified, my hand would tremble so much that the spoon would turn over and the soup would spill onto the table. No matter how desperately I tried to get the soup to my mouth, I would fail every time. Mother would become enraged because I hadn't learned how to use a spoon or a fork in the very few times she had allowed me to eat at the table, so it would end in another beating.

Mother would have her turn beating and kicking me around the house, and then Father would take over. He'd grab me by my hair and lift me over his head and let me drop to the floor. My parents never considered the pain they were inflicting. Not only did they hit me with their hands, they also used belts, sticks, skipping ropes, knives, and broom handles. There were even times when they used a horsewhip.

On the weekends all the housecleaning, water carrying, and wood chopping had to be done on Saturdays because Sunday was the lord's Day, and you were not allowed to do those things then. Mother was very involved in the church and never missed a service. I remember an old man who would run all over, on fire for God, shouting, "God is coming! God is coming!" I was a seven-year-old child. He frightened the daylights out of me. I really thought God was just outside the door waiting to come in. When the preacher came to visit our house, Mother and Father always made it seem like we were a big, happy family. What hypocrites they were!

Sunday dinners always looked and smelled so delicious, but I never got any. The only times I remember getting a decent meal in those years were when company came. Even that happy event would be a double-edged sword because getting a meal would also lead to yet another beating at night or early in the morning hours. Mother was not giving me the freedom to eat a meal at any time, night or day, without a beating.

In later years I found out why church was so important to Mother in those days. More than thirty years had passed since I'd been returned to her and my dad from the foster home. Father told the story of how Mother had asked him to visit the minister in town to see if he could somehow help with getting me back home. Father did as she requested. The minister agreed to help them get their daughter Sandra back if they promised faithfully that they would attend church and live a better life.

Mother didn't want anyone to know the terrible demons she was hiding inside. Her supposed reason for getting me back was that she had come from a Salvation army background, and I'd been placed in a catholic foster home. The man who stepped in to have me returned home was a Pentecostal preacher.

My parents' conversion made big news in the little town of Norris Arm. I remember seeing all the people standing around as the preacher walked Mother and Father through the saltwater of the atlantic Ocean just off the shore of Newfoundland and said, "I now baptize you in the name of the Father, the Son, and the Holy Ghost." Everyone started singing. My parents emerged from the water as pure as new babies, being born again. The song was: "He took my sins away. He took my sins away. And He keeps me singing e-v-e-r-y day."

CHAPTER SEVEN
MOVING TO PETERVIEW

Our family moved to a new home after school was done in the summer of 1967, four months after my eighth birthday. Life in this new town was a little better.

Again we were back to living in a little woodshed, this one belonging to my uncle Zack Brown. He was letting Father use it as a home until Father got something bigger and better for the family to live in. This place was very small, and we were by then a family of eight, with six children. There was no bedroom, just an open space with one bed for the children and one for Mother and Father to sleep in. The table was just a piece of board nailed to one wall. The kids sat on the bed to eat their meals, which were cooked on an old woodstove. There was no running water or indoor bathroom. We got drinking water from uncle Zack's house.

This little place wasn't much better than the house we had moved from in Norris Arm. Father worked hard trying to get a home, but that took time. The little woodshed had to be home for now.

I was happier there. We were around more people, and they came to visit often. Living in my uncle's yard meant they knew everything that went on with our family, so I was treated better than before.

Mother didn't get along with my aunt lily Brown and talked badly about her all the time. But that didn't stop my aunt. She was happy because now she could keep a closer eye on things and see what Mother was really up to. She made it her business to ensure that Mother wasn't beating or starving me. And like my grandparents, aunt lily would give me food. My aunt was a very forward person, and if she had something to say, she said it. Of course, that didn't go over well with Mother, but she knew aunt lily wouldn't back off.

I was now getting more food and fewer beatings, but that doesn't mean they stopped. Weeks after moving into this place, Mother went to get some Sugar Daddy candies that she had put away for the kids, and one was missing. I was in for my usual beating. Mother became enraged and beat me with a stick on both of my hands. My right hand got beaten the worst, leaving it all red. It looked like someone had put a round ball under the skin. It swelled so much that I remember looking at it and not being able to see my fingers.

After the beating was over, I was told, "Get in bed as fast as you can without talking or crying!" That night I felt so sick to my stomach that I threw up all over the bedding. When Mother found me in this mess the next morning, I was ordered to strip the bed and go outside to where she kept the washtub and scrubbing board. I had to wash all the quilts with my bare hands, which were swollen to about twice their normal size from the beating I'd had the night before. Mother stood there without even looking at my hands and said, "Get out there and do what I told you!" My hands hurt terribly as I fetched water from the stream to fill the washtub. Then, with my hands stinging in the water, I scrubbed those big, heavy quilts until they were clean.

While doing this, I noticed a family friend walk by. She was about to pass me when she heard me crying. As she got closer, she could see my hands were badly beaten and very cold. "Sandra," She said, "what happened to your hands? Did your mother do this?" I nodded my head yes. She took my hands out of the cold water and told me to stay there. "I'm going to get Sis," She said.

This lady was aunt lily's sister. I stood there and watched as she ran to her sister's house. In minutes they were both hurrying toward me. The sister stayed outside with me as my aunt lily went inside and demanded answers from Mother. I could hear them both yelling at each other for the longest time. The sister took over washing the quilts as I stood there, scared to death. Now Mother would kill me for sure! There was no way she would let this incident pass without giving me another beating. I stood there crying, in pain, wishing that this lady hadn't walked by and seen me.

Now Mother was outraged because my aunt lily had questioned her treatment of her children. Mother was not about to be put in her place. After the yelling and screaming was over that day and things calmed down, I was ordered by Mother to get back in bed and not to even think about getting anything to eat. Two days went by. Finally I was given a slice of bread with butter. I was being punished because my aunt and her sister had stepped in to help.

Within months of this taking place, we moved again and went to live in the home of Mother's sister, aunt Kathleen, and her family. Their house was a mile or so down the road from where we had been living in uncle Zack's yard. As in uncle Zack's woodshed, there were always

Other people around the house. That's probably why I don't remember any really bad beatings at that time. It was a busy house with two families living together. The older children in both families had to give a helping hand. I didn't mind that. After all, I got to eat with everyone else and play with the other children. Things were starting to look up for me. The freedom of not being beaten made me feel normal for the short time we lived there. But as usual for me in those days, the good times didn't last.

We'd been living at aunt Kathleen's for a few months, and everyone seemed to be getting along well together, but for some reason Mother got mad at her sister and we had to move out again. By this time Father had made a start on a house he was building. However, it still needed a lot of work before it was habitable. Mother said, "We're going to move in and that's it." So there we were again—just one room for a family of eight.

While the rest of the house was being slowly completed, this room would now be our home. The first night we slept there, it was very cold. The rain hit the thin roof covering so hard that my father feared we'd lose it. Finally we got to sleep. The next morning some of us got out of bed with our hair all wet from the rain. Again times were hard for me. I wasn't getting much food to eat, and my freedom was taken away once again. We were back in our own little world, where Mother ran the house and Father was away working. Even when he was home, there wasn't much he could say or do because Mother was the boss. The everyday beatings started again. But people came and went as if things were normal in our home.

In this period Mother was going out every night with her friends. Patty and I would keep house and take care of the little children. On nights when Father wasn't working, he was home helping. But when it came to dealing with Mother, Father was like a little boy. What Mother said went. Father never talked back to her. When she was in a rage, most of the time he just walked outside until she calmed down.

Mother was the love of his life. He did whatever it took to keep her happy. Mother never once had to get out of bed in the morning to get us children ready for school. When Father wasn't working, he was always up before daybreak to get the fire going in the winter. When it was really cold outside, Father would stay up all night stoking the woodstove to keep the house warm. He would melt the frozen butter in the oven or on top of the stove to put on the bread for our lunches.

Father's inconsistent behaviour really confused me. I didn't know what to think of him. Mother would go out most every night, and then he would talk about what Mother was doing to me. "Someday, she'll have to pay for all the hardship she's put you through, my dear," He would say. "Her day will come. You can bet on that. God almighty will make her suffer." I would stand there thinking: What about your part in this?

I remember that sometimes there were big sores on my legs that hurt terribly, and they would break open on their own. When that happened Father would put boiling water in a pop bottle and use it to draw out the infection in the sores. He would keep the boiling water there until the pus and blood were drawn out. "Now that's how you get rid of a boil," Father would say. Both of my legs got infected from Father doing this. My parents tried to clean the infections up in hopes they might clear up on their own, but nothing worked. They got worse. Finally Mother took me to the doctor and I was admitted again to hospital for three weeks.

I was so happy in the hospital, being bathed and waited on and fed three meals every day. I remember lying in bed with my legs in a big thing that looked like a tent. It was to protect them from the bed covers. With a smile on my face I would wait for the meal trays to come around. I was so happy to get food, knowing that it wouldn't be taken from me before I could eat it and that I wouldn't get beaten.

The nurses would come and fix me up so I could eat my meals, cranking up the head of my bed. The beds were high, but that didn't bother me at all. I was happy to have a real bed of my own to sleep in at night, without anyone pulling on me for some unknown reason. A bed of my own was a luxury beyond anything I could have hoped for. I prayed it would never end.

Mother explained my hospital stay to friends by saying I had a rash from wearing knitted slippers. I've never had a rash or eczema in my life. But that didn't matter to me at the time, and neither did the needles, the blood work, or being confined to bed. My legs were so badly infected that my doctor didn't want me out walking around the hospital floors. That was okay with me because, for the few short weeks I was there, this little girl was very happy. The Botwood Hospital no longer exists, but the love and care the hospital staff gave me will forever remain in my thoughts.

Back home, when my parents had company, I'd crawl into bed thinking maybe Mother would forget about me if I was out of the way. I'd try to get to sleep as fast as I could, hoping that maybe that night I would be spared the pain of another beating. Many nights I'd be fast asleep before the visitors left. But somehow, over the course of the day, Mother always managed to find a reason to get angry with me when our family was alone again. Maybe earlier, when she'd brought out a meal for her friends, she'd noticed that some cookies were missing, or a piece of cake. Whether I was guilty of taking it or not, Mother always seemed to blame me.

One night she was going to put a bottle of beets on the table but couldn't find it. As soon as the company was gone, I was pulled from bed. Father forced my mouth open with his hands to see if I had eaten those beets. To this day I don't recall eating them, but Father said my tongue was red, so automatically I was to be punished for this crime. My parents found an extension cord and beat me with it. Every blow from the cord made me bleed. When they finally let me go, I was unable to move.

Sometimes, shouting, they'd say what it was they thought I'd done wrong, but many times not a word was spoken. They just beat me for some imagined wrong. I'd be pulled from my sleep, beaten, and then put back to bed again. I never knew why they hated me so much. The beatings were so frequent that I seldom got a full night's sleep. Come morning, Father would pull me out by my feet or he would yell, "Get out of the fucking bed now before I come in there!" Wasting no time, I'd jump out of bed as fast as I could to get ready for school. Many days I'd go to school with no socks on my feet and nothing on my hands to keep them warm. One time my fingers got frozen, and Father had to take my hands and put them in ice cold water to bring them back to life.

At that time there was no school bus running, so we walked to and from school. It was more than a mile from where we lived. The winters were cold and the snow was deep. Some days the wind would blow the snow around the road, making it hard for us to see where we were going. Sometimes we couldn't even see in front of us. The wind would almost sweep me off my feet.

On break from school at lunchtime, I'd have to go to the frozen water hole and chop through the ice to get water to fill the washer. After I was done, Mother would give me a small piece of bread for my lunch. I would almost always go back to school very hungry.

Things were like hell for me at home, but school wasn't much better. I was the outcast at home and at school. The entire school made fun of me every day. I hated them and just wanted to die. I didn't want Mother's voice ringing in my ears day after day, saying over and over, "You'll never be any good to anyone. No one will ever want you." Eventually I started to think and say to myself, Yes, Mother, you're right. Why don't you just kill me and have it over with?

I was never allowed to watch movies as the other children in the house did. I would listen from the bedroom as they watched and talked about the show on the television. Father loved cowboy shows and tarzan. I remember our first tv because Joey and Patty were always talking happily about the movies and cartoons as we walked to school. Sometimes Mother would make popcorn in the cooking pot on the old woodstove for the children to eat as they enjoyed their movies. I would sit on the bedroom floor and listen to the sound of the popcorn popping. Night after night I'd cry. I wanted so much to watch tv with the family. Mother never once gave a thought to letting me sit with them.

Life in that home was not easy for any of the children who lived there. We all got our turn at being beaten and yelled at over the years. But it was much harder for me. I never understood why Father protected my brother and sisters from Mother's hands and not me.

One time Mother gave Patty money to go to the post office after school to pay a bill. When she got home, Mother asked for the change. Patty said there wasn't any. She insisted that the lady hadn't given any change back. Mother became furious with her and was going to beat her with a big stick of wood. But when

Mother raised her arm to hit her, Father grabbed the stick out of Mother's hand and said, "You're not touching her. If she said she got no change back, I believe her." Father took Patty back to the post office with him and asked the lady about where the change went. The lady checked her till and saw that she was ten dollars over from her daily intake. Though Father never defended me, I was happy for Patty that he was home to protect her that day.

Once Mother went to put some cheese on the table for dinner. As she unwrapped the block of cheese, she noticed someone had taken a bite out of it. Again I was the one Mother blamed. "Get it out here!" She yelled to Father. "I'll give the like of that biting into the cheese like that."

Father pulled me out and ripped my top. I was very scared and started crying without even knowing what was taking place. I repeated over and over, "I didn't do it!" I didn't know what I was being accused of, but I figured I must have done something wrong. Holding my hands in front of my face for protection, I cried, "Mom, I'll be good. I won't do it again!"

Father told Mother to hold off hitting me for a moment. "I'll prove she's lying," He said. Father was a smart man. He took the block of cheese with the bite mark and compared it with my bite. My front tooth had a piece missing from the corner. The bite mark in the cheese was straight across and matched with Joey's teeth. Father was so sure he'd caught me in a lie that day. Mother was so crazy that she beat me anyway. Over the years i've often wondered why Joey never got a beating for biting into the cheese that day.

I often got beatings for things the other children did wrong. My younger sister Ellie was always blaming me for things. Whenever her turn came to do the dishes, even if I wasn't in the same room as her, she would cry and say, "Mom! Sandra said she's not going to wash the dishes."

Mother would yell and say, "The Goddamn Thing will do the dishes."

Ellie would look at me and laugh and say, "Ha-ha! I don't have to do the dishes." She would always get her own way when she didn't want to do something. By this time she was Mommy's pet. Even if she cut herself it was my fault. Many times on our way to school, Patty, Joey, and I would push Ellie in the snowbank because she was always crying to Mommy about something. We gave her a new name, Big Baby, because she got away with everything.

There were times when Mother would beat Patty and Joey, but they never got beaten as badly or as often as I did. They don't have scars on their bodies like I do.

Mother always wore Father's shoes on her feet at home. There were times when she would throw me on the floor and jump on me violently with her three-hundred-and-fiftypound body. One time she came down on me so hard that the heel of father's shoe went through my left thigh and broke the skin wide open, leaving the heel print of the shoe in my skin.

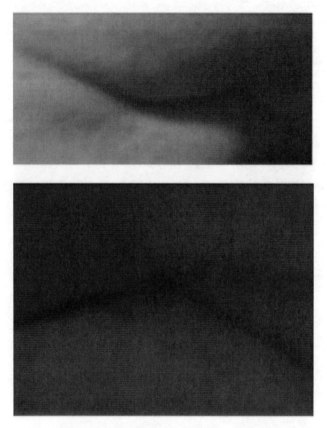

Photos of scar that I will carry for the rest of my life.

Although the scar has blurred over the years, the memory of that day will live on. It is a lasting reminder of Mother's violent attacks.

CHAPTER EIGHT
STEALING

Sometimes at school, when I was in grade three, my classmates would be busy doing their school work, and I'd ask the teacher if I could go to the bathroom. After leaving the classroom, I would stop at the coat locker and steal candy and gum from my classmates' jacket pockets. I'd take it with me into the bathroom and eat it before going back to class. I did this for a few months until the teacher started asking me if I was taking candy and gum from my classmates. I told her, "No, Miss, it wasn't me."

One afternoon I took a row of gum balls from a girl's pocket. There were five big gumballs of different colours. They were so good! I had so much fun chewing into all that gum. But I forgot to clean my mouth before heading back to class. As I entered the classroom and walked toward my desk, I noticed all my classmates staring at me. Some of them were smiling. I was puzzled but sat down at my desk and quietly got back to my work. The teacher looked at me and said, "Sandra, please step outside the classroom. I'd like to have a word with you."

Parts of my body tightened up as I got out of my seat and began to walk toward her. I knew if the teacher called me outside the classroom it meant trouble. Once we got outside, she started to ask me questions about why I was stealing from my classmates. I told her I did it because I was so hungry and confessed that I hadn't eaten in days. She looked at me with tears rolling down my face and said, "I have to bring you to the principal's office."

Slowly I walked behind her, dragging my feet and trying to dry my eyes as we walked. The teacher knocked on the principal's door. Then I heard his voice saying, "come in!" My teacher opened the door to his office and told him that I had been stealing things from the other kids' pockets. The principal then looked at me and said, "Sit down, Sandra." There I was, sitting on the chair with my head down, not knowing what was coming next. I told him I had taken the candy because I was hungry and didn't get much to eat at home. The principal then picked up the phone to call my mother and tell her what was going on. I began to cry, telling him that if he called my mother, she would kill me for stealing at school.

He said, "Sandra, I can't have you stealing from the other children."

Shivering with fear, I then begged him, "Please don't call my mother!" I went on to tell him how much my mother beat me, and that she would let me go for days without food or water.

Putting the phone down, he said, "Is that right?"

I said, "Yes, sir." The principal told me to go back to class. But if it happened again, he warned me, "I will call your mother. Do you hear me?"

With tears of shame and relief in my eyes, I said, "Yes, sir!"

While I was thankful he hadn't called my mother that day, a part of me was wishing he had called someone else.

Maybe that person would have gotten me out of my mother's house. Over the years I've thought about that day often and never understood why the principal or God or somebody didn't step in and get help for me. I kept going to school as if nothing had happened. Soon that day was just a bad memory like most days in my life.

I was now at the end of grade three. Being out of school meant more beatings and less to eat at home. In September I was placed in an opportunity class. This was a class for children who were having trouble with school work and were a little slow in understanding things. That was the best thing that ever happened to me as a child. My teacher for that class was so nice and very soft-spoken. She helped me with my school work and took time to show me how it was done without yelling at me. I did a lot of nice things in this class, such as sewing, arts and crafts, and many outdoor activities like gardening, playing outdoor games, and identifying trees and birds.

The opportunity class was a class of about ten children. We all knew each other because we'd gone to the same school for years. This new class was good for us, and we learned a lot from being there. We all loved our teacher because she did so many nice things for us. Sometimes she even took us to her house after school and gave us pizza and pop. I didn't understand why I stole from her, but stealing had become a big thing for me by then, and I couldn't stop taking money from her.

One time I took twenty dollars and got myself a new pair of running shoes. When I got home, Mother asked me where the shoes had come from. I told her the teacher had given them to me. Mother never questioned me about the shoes again because my teacher was always doing nice things for the kids in her class. Her students were like her family.

I was now stealing just about every day—nothing big most of the time, just change. Every time the teacher would leave the classroom for some reason, I would go through her purse. Watching carefully as the other children played with toys, I would rapidly work my way toward the teacher's desk and go through her purse to take some money. Usually it would be only twenty-five cents. I'd be very happy with that because I could get a bag of chips, a chocolate bar, ice cream, and candy. After school was over for the day, I would run off to the store and buy chips and candy with the money. I'd share them with the other kids in my class and also give my brother and sister some of my treats so they wouldn't tell Mother that I was stealing.

Having treats to share was helping me make friends with a lot of kids in school, and that made me feel good about myself. Being liked and having friends was really important to someone like me. Now that I had friends, I didn't have to listen to them calling me names—as long as I was giving them things.

My friend Nancy was really nice to me even if I didn't have anything to give away. She was always there beside me, no matter what. We walked to school together. Sometimes Mother would send me to the store to pick up the things she needed. Nancy would come with me and we would play games. One of them was called You can't catch Me! We would run after each other like crazy. I never could catch Nancy, but we sure had fun playing that game.

Nancy never called me names as all the other kids did. At times she would fight other kids when they picked on me. I always felt safe with Nancy around. She was like my bodyguard.

Often when I got home from the store, Mother would yell at me and ask, "What took you so long?" I always told her the storekeeper was very busy. Sometimes she would beat me anyway for lying to her about being gone so long to the store.

I was now nine years old. On a good day I was given a small portion of vegetables. The other children in our home were given some of everything that was cooked for that meal. I loved the smell of chicken. Some days there was roast beef with Yorkshire pudding and gravy. My mouth would water as I was ordered to stand at the table and eat my little serving of vegetables.

One day after school I decided to go and visit aunt Doris, Mother's sister. I knew if she was home, she would give me something to eat. Mother wouldn't have to know anything about it. That was one of my ways of getting food. When I got to aunt Doris's house, she had gone out. My eyes fell upon her purse, sitting there on the table. I remember thinking how hungry I was and how much I wanted something to eat.

I opened the purse, looked inside, and saw money. So I took it. I ran outside and up the road. When I got around to the front of the school, no one could see me. I stopped to take a look at how much money was in my hand. Wow, I thought, seven dollars! That's a lot of money. I imagined all the good food I could buy with it. I held it tight in my hand and hurried off to the store. I got inside the store and didn't know what to get with all that money. A thousand things were going through my mind.

All at once I knew what I would do. Mother needed milk, bread, and butter. There weren't any in the house. I thought if I got those things for Mother, she would love me for doing it. I decided that if she asked me where the money had come from, I'd tell her I found it on the school grounds.

I was feeling very happy as I walked out of the store with bags in my arms. Then I heard a voice calling, "Sandra, come here!" I looked across the street toward the gas bar and saw my aunt Doris in her car. I walked over to where she was. When I got closer to her car, she ordered me to get in. "Now!" She said, as she reached over to open the door. After I got in, she asked me if I'd been at her house.

I said, "No, I just came from school."

She told me that I'd been seen coming out of her house. So I confessed that I had gone over to visit her.

She then asked me, "Did you take money from my house?"

I denied it.

Yelling this time, aunt Doris asked the question again. I admitted to taking the money and begged her not to tell Mother about what I'd done. She made me go to the store to explain to the storekeeper that I had stolen the money and get her money back.

After I gave her the money, she pulled me by the arm, put me in her car, and drove straight to my house. She told Mother everything. I knew I was in real trouble this time. I was shivering with fear as Mother talked with her sister, knowing that the very minute my aunt left, I would get a beating for this crime that I had committed. I tried to prepare my body as I waited for my punishment.

As soon as my aunt left, Mother turned on me as I'd expected, screaming over and over again: "You've really done it this time! I'll teach you not to take money from anyone ever again." She yelled to my father to bring her something hard. Father pulled his belt off real fast. Mother yelled, "That's not hard enough! I want to teach her a lesson."

Father left to go get something harder for Mother to beat me with. As I stood there waiting, Mother told me to get my clothes off. By the time Father returned, I was standing before Mother naked and shivering with fear. Father handed Mother a whip that he used on the horses.

I watched as he walked to his chair as I had seen him do so many times before and said, "come here to me." Grabbing me by the hair, he pulled my head down between his knees, holding my arms tight in his hands. I knew there was no escape. He said to Mother, "Now give it to her!" My brother and sister, who were standing nearby, watching in silence, were ordered to hold my legs as Mother whipped me over and over again.

I remember getting weak. My stomach churned as blow after blow hit my back, upper arms, and legs. I wanted to die that day. It seemed as if they would never let me go. I felt each blow of the whip cut my skin. Finally Mother stopped and Father let me go. I tried with all my might to stand on my feet and make my way back to the bedroom. My body wouldn't hold itself up. I tried to take a step but staggered and fell to the floor. I was too weak to move. I remember hearing Father's voice saying, "Now if that's not enough, I'll teach you to listen. The next time, we'll whip you with a cato'-nine-tails."

My back was bleeding badly from that beating. I could neither lie on my back for a long time nor sit up straight in my desk at school. My teacher asked me many times if I was okay. Holding back the tears, my answer was always, "Yes, Miss, I'm fine." I didn't dare tell my teacher, fearing Mother would find out that I had said something.

It's a memory that will be with me for the rest of my life. I know that what I did was wrong, but I know, too, that I didn't do it to hurt my aunt Doris. It was because I was hungry and needed something to eat.

I don't believe anyone has the right to hurt someone else the way they punished me that day. The fact that it was my mother's sister that I had taken the money from didn't help matters. Mother was always so proud and spoke very highly of her family. She would go on about how they didn't want for anything, how her father worked hard all his life to put food on the table and clothing on their backs, and how they were never on welfare. "Not like the Browns," She would say. "I never saw dirt until I met your father."

Mother would always put my father's family down so much. It was so unfair. Whenever she needed help, Father's family was there for us. Maybe they didn't have much, but what little they had they freely shared. I will cherish the memories of my father's family forever. I am certain in my heart that it's because of Father's family that I am alive today to write this story about my life in hell.

Another memory I have is of being home from school for lunch on a warm summer day. I got my slice of bread but was still very hungry. I wanted seconds but I was too afraid to ask for more. Heading to the door, I suddenly noticed a piece of bread on the floor. I picked it up and shoved it inside the red pants that I was wearing that day, hoping to save it for later. Then I noticed Mother looking at me. She didn't say anything because there was company in the house that day. So I returned the bread to the floor, knowing that if I were to take the bread and eat it, Mother would be even more furious.

That afternoon at school, as I sat in class, all I could think of was the beating that I was going to get when I got home for picking up the bread. I kept watching the big clock on the wall, worried about when the school bell would ring. On my way home that day all I could think of was the punishment that was waiting for me for trying to take that piece of bread. As I walked slowly with my head down, I thought of jumping in front of an oncoming car. I looked for a piece of glass to cut myself enough that I would have to be taken to the hospital. Maybe the doctor would keep me there for a few days. But no cars came, and I found no glass. Reaching the driveway to our home, I saw an axe on the chopping block. I picked it up and placed my hand on the block. Turning my head to the side, I brought the axe down across my left fingers.

I made one good chop with that axe, hoping my fingers were gone. As I looked down to bring the axe away from my hand, I saw blood running down the chopping block. I was thinking my fingers were buried in blood. I went inside the house to where Mother was standing. A path of blood fell behind me as I walked. She grabbed my arm, pulled me over to the sink, and ran cold water over my hand, discovering a huge gash there. My fingers were cut halfway through. I had thought that I'd be going to the hospital, but Father had another idea. His remedy was to glue my fingers together with myrrh that came from the thorny commiphora trees.

"That's better than any bandage," My father said. Mother then wrapped my hand with cloth.

This happened in 1968. I was nine years old. Despite the wounds I'd already received from the axe, Mother beat me with a stick over and over again that evening. I can still hear her words: "I'll mark you to your grave!" The cuts bled for many days afterward.

Some evenings, after school, Mother would give me a note to go to the store. The things I bought were to be marked on a store tape, and Mother would pay for them when Father got his cheque at the end of the month. I was always happy to do this because it gave me another way of stealing food, and Mother didn't find out about it right away. I would pick up everything that was on the list and always add something for myself. I would eat it on my way back home. Most of the time it would be some cooked ham, six slices in a pack. I would rip it open. With the juice running down my chin and hands, I wasted no time in eating that ham. I knew it would be a long time before I'd get to enjoy a meal like that again.

I would walk into the house, put the bags of food on the table as if I were completely innocent, and wait for Mother to yell at me to get into my room. I'd go in the room with my belly full and the taste of cooked ham still in my mouth.

By the age of ten, stealing food had become my way of life. Mother didn't know anything about it. By then I was going to school in a new town that we had to travel to by bus. Every day that I got on that bus, the kids would tease me and call me names. "Shorty" Was what they called me the most. "Oh, Shorty! You're too short to sit down." Some of the boys would put their foot out as I walked by and trip me. Then they would all laugh and say, "Get up, Shorty! What are you doing down there?"

At school I would often hide stolen things outside in the long, uncut grass. Because it was close to the outside walls of the school, it was a good hiding place. No one ever looked there. I was beginning to get really good at stealing. I would drift off to sleep every night with a smile on my face, thinking about what I was going to steal the next day. I was getting in bigger and deeper. I was no longer thinking about school work. My every thought was about stealing food and much more. Stealing became the centre of my life.

In my teenage years I graduated from stealing food to footwear, and then to makeup and pretty things to wear. Whatever I wanted, I got. There was no stopping me. I would go into a store with just enough money to buy a package of Kool-aid, which cost six cents at the time. I would come out with pork chops, bacon, roast beef, chicken, cheese slices, and ground beef inside my coat. When I got home at the end of a shopping day, I'd have something for everyone in the family. There'd be new outfits for the children to wear back to school, things they needed to do their school work, and treats for school. We were now living like rich people, wanting for nothing. There was nothing too big or too small for me to steal.

By the time I turned twenty, I was a professional thief, stealing every day, not just for my family. I was now taking outside orders from other people, and we're talking big money. Stealing was just like a full-time job for me. I was busy filling orders every day, keeping all my customers happy, making sure they placed more orders. Christmas was an especially good time of the year to make money. There was no end to the orders that came in each day.

I became so good at stealing over the years that I had people approach me to teach them how. I was also becoming a modern, female robin Hood. Many times I went into my friends' homes and saw they had no food to feed their children. I would leave without saying a word, go to a store, steal food, and bring it back to their house. To me the risk was worth it just to witness the little kids smiling when they saw the food.

This went on for many years—until I was in my thirties. I remember the first time I walked into a store and paid for things. I felt so proud of myself. It felt good not having to look over my shoulder to see if anyone was following me.

CHAPTER NINE
LOSING MY EYE

I have another vivid memory. It was the summer of 1967, when I was eight years old. The day was beautiful, hot, and sunny. I was walking past my mother, who was standing beside the kitchen cupboards. I don't remember saying or doing anything to upset her that day, but just as I walked by her, she picked up the ever-present belt and hit me across the face with it. The buckle hit me in the left eye. Pain seared through my face. Mother screamed at me and said, "I'll teach you not to look at me with those sly eyes!" Water came from my eye and down my face. It wouldn't stop. Mother kept yelling and telling me to stop crying. I tried to tell her I wasn't crying, but she didn't believe me and wouldn't hear a thing I had to say, then or in the days to come.

I tried many times after that day to tell my parents about the pain in my left eye and how I couldn't see from it, but they both ignored me. For many months I tried to convince them that my eye was seriously damaged. I was having terrible headaches and the infection was there for anyone to see. The eye would fill up with pus until it ran down my face. It was very painful.

The headaches went on for two years and so did the infections. Finally my father decided to put me through a test to see if I was lying about not seeing from my eye. Father covered the good eye with a brown envelope and told me to walk into the bedroom and back out to him again. Knowing the house so well, I did this with almost no trouble at all. I tried hard not to trip or bump into things because I was afraid of upsetting them. When I returned to the kitchen, Father said, "See? I knew there was nothing wrong with your eye!"

With tears in my eyes I said, "Yes, Dad, it's very painful and it's hurting me all the time now." But my soft-spoken words didn't matter to him or my mother, who was standing nearby. As Father took off his belt, I began to tremble with fear, knowing there was no way out. Mother ordered me to get my clothes off as fast as I could. I was ten years old, standing before my father with nothing on my body. Blow after blow from the belt hit my flesh. I wanted so much for them to believe me and care, but that was impossible for them to do.

From that day forward there was no mention about the eye. Weeks turned into months. The pain got to the point where I would close my eyes every night and pray, "God, somehow let Mother see that my eye is really hurt and I am blind in it. Please, God, make it possible. I don't know if I can take another day of this pain."

I'd lie in an old bed, without a warm blanket, holding my head tight in my hands because the pain was so bad. I would have done anything to make this pain go away. As months passed, the pain got much worse. There was no escape. I prayed night after night, "God, you must help me." I was not allowed to talk about my pain because Mother didn't want to hear about it. If I was caught crying, I'd be beaten again.

I fought to somehow survive those headaches. I hoped and prayed that they would go away soon. As time went on, I kept praying for a miracle to happen so my blindness would be exposed. Finally, in October 1969, that miracle occurred. I was ten years old. My grandmother was taking care of me, my four sisters, and one brother. Mother was in the hospital giving birth to twins—two more baby sisters, beautiful like two little dolls.

One night, as I was getting ready for bed at the home of my Grandmother Burt (my mother's mother), the pain was now in my right eye as well. I remember going to the bathroom to clean liquid and pus from that eye and found it to be very irritated, but I was afraid to tell Grandmother about it. Mother had given me her order long before going into the hospital: I was not about to mess up by telling Grandmother Burt that there was something wrong with my eye.

Just as on every other night at Grandmother's house, although my eye ached, I was happy to get into a beautiful, warm bed and get a full night's sleep without getting pulled out in the middle of the night and beaten.

And the food at Grandmother's house was so good! I always got the same as the other children. I was never excluded or ordered to leave. My aunt Daisy would help me with my homework every night before going to bed. I was now in grade three. The work was hard, but with aunt Daisy helping me those few nights when we stayed there, I felt so smart. For the first time in school I got a hundred percent on my math test. I was so proud of myself and so thankful for aunt Daisy's help.

One morning, when I woke up, I couldn't open my right eye. It was stuck shut. The pus and liquid that had drained as I slept had dried and stuck the eyelids together. I got out of bed that morning and made my way toward the bedroom door, but not knowing the house well, I walked into a wall. My grandmother heard the noise and came to ask what was wrong with me. I told her that I couldn't see anything out of my right eye.

"What are you talking about, 'you can't see'?" She asked me.

Up to this point, my grandmother had no idea there was anything wrong with my left eye. Grandmother told aunt Daisy to take me into the bathroom and clean my eye. My aunt took my hand and said, "Sandra, walk with me." After the mess was cleaned out of my eye, I was able to see again with my right eye, but the pain was still there.

When Mother returned home from the hospital, Grandmother told her to take me to see a doctor. A few weeks went by. Mother finally broke down and took me to the Botwood Hospital. I remember that day as if it happened yesterday. It turned out I had an infection called pink eye, which took about one week to go away. But the doctor also gave me a test to see how good my vision was in both eyes. After completing the test, he asked me to sit in the waiting room because he wanted to talk to my mother alone. As I sat outside the office and waited on the wooden chair that day, I heard the doctor questioning my mother about how my left eye had gotten to be this way, and how long the sight had been gone from my left eye. I'll never forget how I felt when Mother told the doctor I'd been hit by a snowball in the schoolyard, but she hadn't known that I couldn't see from that eye.

Thank God, the doctor didn't believe my mother that day. I overheard him say to Mother, "Mrs. Brown, that injury didn't happen even remotely the way you said. There was no snowball." Unfortunately, he said, he couldn't prove just how it had happened. I wanted to go back into the office and scream that she was lying and she was responsible. But knowing I had to go home and live with her, I didn't dare say anything.

The doctor set up an appointment with an ophthalmologist in Gander, the first of many eye appointments. Within weeks I was off to see this new doctor. After more tests, just like the first doctor he said there was nothing he could do for my eye. It was too late. The eye could not be saved.

This new doctor set up an appointment with another doctor, in St. John's. It was an eight-hour bus ride to get there. On my first trip to see this new doctor, an optical surgeon, in the summer of 1971, he ran a number of further tests. After he was done, he talked to my mother about his findings. He said the eye had received such a heavy blow and had been left untreated for so long that it was now wasted away on the inside. If the eye had been treated back when the injury had occurred, he told her, he could have saved it. "But now the eye has to be removed. It's dead and has been for a long time. The child will never have sight in that eye again."

I thought: Thank God! Yes, I was scared, hearing that my eye would have to be removed, but knowing the pain would be gone after the surgery made me feel much better. The next morning we got back on the bus and returned home to wait for a call from the optical surgeon, to get an appointment to have the eye removed. Within a few weeks the call came through and a date was set to go back for the surgery.

As family and friends came to visit at this time, they asked my mother what had happened to Sandra's eye and why it had to be taken out. My Mother would tell them that the doctor in Gander had given her the wrong eye drops, and that was how Sandra had lost her sight in that eye.

In September 1971 Mother and I were on the bus again, heading back to St. John's—this time to the Janeway Hospital, to have the eye removed. The eight-hour trip with my mother and a family friend seemed to take forever. I got sick whenever we had to take this trip, but the bus driver was always nice. He would pull off the road to let me off for a few minutes. But it wasn't always the bus ride that made me sick. The thought of having my eye taken out was very frightening. We got into town at night and took a taxi to the red cross Hostel, where we stayed. I tried hard to sleep that night but couldn't stop thinking about the surgery. Soon morning came and we were on our way to the hospital. After I was admitted, Mother got the next bus back home.

I was eleven years old, all alone and very frightened. I remember as they took me down and got me ready for surgery, there wasn't anyone there that I knew. Just before they put me to sleep, a man I'd never seen before stood at my bedside. I remember him asking if he could pray for me. With tears in my eyes I said, "Yes sir!" As he was praying, I went to sleep. After the surgery was over, the first person I remember seeing was this man standing at my bedside. When I think about this man and how he stayed beside me throughout my frightening time, I imagine him as an angel sent from God.

They removed my eye. But despite this loss, again I found the stay in the hospital warm and welcoming. The staff took very good care of me. The food was delicious, my bed was very soft, and I felt so clean after a long bath in the big tub. I remember a nurse giving me a can of tooth powder and a toothbrush to clean my teeth, but I didn't know how to do it because I'd never had a toothbrush. The nurse was nice and taught me. I didn't like the taste of the tooth powder in my mouth, but it made my mouth feel clean.

After a few days in the hospital, I got to sit at the little table and chairs that were there for the young children. I would sit there and help the little children with their toys and colour pictures with them. The nurse would say, "You're a big help, Sandra." I would give them a little smile and say, "Yes, I take care of my little sisters and brother at home, and I love babies."

After a week's stay at the hospital, I was released to go home for six weeks until I would return to St. John's to have a glass eye fitting. My first four weeks of being home, I had to wear a gauze pad to cover my eye. I was to wear this until my return to St. John's. But Mother said there was no money to get any more gauze. So for the following two weeks I walked around and attended school with nothing covering my eye socket. It made me look very odd, having it open like that. The kids at school teased me and called me ugly names like One eye Dick and Breta Brown's Monster. This name-calling went on until I left school. It made me so mad and so ashamed that I began to hate myself and didn't want to go to school. I didn't want to be around people at all. I felt like a monster and thought of myself as one.

When the six-week period was up, Mother, a family friend, and I set out to get my new eye. I was so happy on this eight-hour bus trip, thinking about getting my new eye. I kept thinking that the kids at school wouldn't be making fun of me anymore. But this trip turned out to be a disappointing one. When we got to the office and talked to the doctor, he said that I had developed an infection from having the eye exposed. He advised Mother to stay in town for a few days, just to give this infection time to go away. Mother said we couldn't stay away from home that long because she had small children at home to care for. The doctor said, "Then bring Sandra back to see me in two weeks." He then looked at me with a wink. "I think she'll be ready for her eye at that time." Off we went again, back home.

Finally, after the two weeks, I was sitting in this little office again and waiting to get my new eye. The doctor came in and sat down beside me. He started to look through the glass eyes.

"Wow!" I said. "I never thought there were so many eye colours, sizes, and different shapes."

As he opened more and more boxes of eyes, I began to feel sick. It seemed as if all those eyes were staring at me. It was scary. I was trying not to look at the doctor. He kept trying to fit eye after eye into my head. It was so hard to find the right colour. Finally he found one to match my good eye, and soon it was fitted. The doctor took Mother into a room and showed her how to take the eye out and clean it. Then he showed her how to put it back in. This would have to be done every day for the rest of my life. The doctor went on to tell Mother that if the eye wasn't kept clean, it could get infected. Infection could even lead to cancer over time.

The first morning we were home, Mother gave me a broken mirror and said, "Here. Go and make sure you clean that eye good." There I was, eleven years old, trying to do a job that my mother had been trained to do. Mother didn't even take the time to show me how it had to be done or help me in any way. I cleaned the eye the best way I knew how and put it back in place. The first few weeks were very hard as I looked at that eye being slowly pulled from my head. Having to remove and clean a glass eye every day for the rest of my life made me sick at first.

Because I was just cleaning it with soap, the eye was always infected, and it was never treated or seen by a doctor. I would have to leave the eye out to let the infection clear up, which might take weeks and maybe even months. It didn't take much for the eye to get infected. Things like smoke from the woodstove, dust off the floor, cold wind, and salt water from the beach would set it off.

I was so embarrassed to have to go to school without a patch or bandage over the hole where my eye had been removed. Once again I was an open target for the children at school to tease and bully. I heard their cutting words over and over in my head. "Here comes Sandra Brown with her glass eye!"

I just wanted to disappear and never be seen or heard from again. I wanted to kill all those kids, and my mother, for making me feel so ugly. Each day I prayed and hoped that tomorrow would never come. Day after day I endured the name-calling at school, the beatings at home, and going hungry.

That glass eye became a continual reminder of my childhood abuse and will remain so for the rest of my life. To this day, the first thing I have to do every morning is remove the eye and clean it.

Over the years I've learned how to take care of the eye properly. It has to be changed and a new one fitted every five to seven years. As I grow older, the eye socket changes, and the old glass eye doesn't fit properly anymore. Getting a new glass eye has changed so much over the years. Now I go into the office and see the new eye being made. I sit and watch the work being done right in front of me. At the end of the day I walk out wearing my new eye. No more drawers or boxes being pulled out and eyes of every colour and size looking up at me.

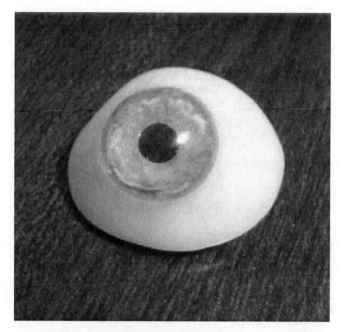

Photo of my glass eye.

I am thankful that the inside muscles of my eye weren't permanently damaged. The first few years after losing my eye, I noticed that there were no tears in that eye. But over the years that changed, and I now have tears again.

I've learned to deal with my glass eye over the years. It's just part of my everyday life. There are still some things I can't take part in, like playing sports. I've got to be very careful when driving my car, making sure I look to both sides at any crosswalk. I can't ride a bike on a busy street. Sometimes in shopping malls I bump into other shoppers because I can't see anyone on my left side.

I often joke with my friends sometimes about how it's a good thing I only have one eye because I already see far more than I want to, when it comes to dealing with things of this world. The other saying I have is: "Don't worry! I'll keep an eye out for you." I learned over the years that it's better to joke and try to come to terms with things than to get upset and let them eat away at you a little each day. Nothing can ever give me back the eye that Mother destroyed so long ago.

Do I miss all the things I can't do because of my eye? No, because I never did them. Do I get upset at times? Yes. Do I wonder what it would be like to see with both eyes? Yes. Do I wonder what I would have looked like if I hadn't lost my eye? Yes. Did my children ever see me with my eye out? No, never. Do I like what I see when I take my eye out for cleaning? No. I try not to look at myself. Do I hate my mother? No. I just want her to feel my pain.

Did I ever ask Mother why she hit me and if she felt badly for destroying my eyesight? Yes. Mother's words were, "You deserved what you got."

In the summer of 2003, in a room of twenty people, Mother cried on my shoulder and said she was sorry. But her words meant nothing to me. After all those years of wondering why, dealing with pain, hiding scars, blaming myself, and wishing I wasn't born, Mother's saying she was sorry was just another slap in the face.

You see, she didn't mean a word she said. Her confession was all about making herself look good in the eyes of others. Mother never once sent me a note, never once took time to give me a call. My children got no christmas gifts from her. Birthdays came and went unacknowledged. Nothing, not even a card, after all those years.

For fifty years I wanted to be Mother's daughter. In November 2011 I wrote her out of my life. She's now just a woman called Mother. In my heart there's no love, no hate, no feeling. I feel nothing for the monster called Mother.

CHAPTER TEN

TEENAGE SHAME

One of my worst memories is of an event that occurred when I was eleven. It was a beautiful Saturday evening, and both of my parents were away. I was home taking care of my younger brothers and sisters when an older male friend of the family dropped by to see my father. I told him that my parents were out for the evening, and that I didn't know when they were coming home. I could tell by the smell of his breath that he was drunk, and he couldn't stand or walk around our house without staggering.

He didn't leave when I asked him to. Instead he just stood there and kept looking at me as I went about the house doing my chores. At some point I went into the bedroom for something. After I got inside the room, I heard sounds behind me. Then the door closed with a loud noise. I turned my head, and over my shoulder I saw that the drunk man had followed me into the bedroom.

I yelled and told him to get out of the bedroom. "There's nothing in here for you," I told him. He reached out and pulled me into him. He started to kiss me on the lips. I tried to pull away, but he was a big man, and all my pushing got me nowhere. I was very frightened and tried frantically to escape, but my attempts to get away had no effect on him. He continued his assault, pulling my underwear off and pushing my body onto the bed.

I screamed and kicked at him but he didn't stop there. He kept touching my body all over and saying, "Oh! You feel so good. I'm not going to hurt you. Just lie still and open your legs for me. I'm going to make you feel real good. You'll like the feeling." He then took my hand and pulled it down, making me touch his penis. "Here, just feel that," He said. "I'll teach you what to do. It'll get real hard. Come on now, you like playing with it, don't you? Here, just rub it a few times."

Crying, I pulled my hand away and told him, "It's dirty! I'll get into trouble, when my mother finds out about this."

"No, you won't," He said. "No one will tell your mother about this."

I was just a small child—only eleven. This big man was now lying on top of me, trying to get his penis inside me. I kept pushing and kicking, struggling to get away from him. But he wouldn't stop. I could feel his penis harden as he rubbed himself on my tiny body. There was nothing I could do to stop him. He had me pinned to the bed and I couldn't move. He raped me.

As I lay on the bed, my body became numb. I could hear the sound of my brother's voice calling as he knocked frantically at the bedroom door, "come out, Sandra! Come out of the room!" But he couldn't get in to help. The man had pushed the dresser up against the bedroom door.

After he was done raping and doing these terrible things to me, the man just got up, opened the bedroom door without saying a word, and left the house. I was terrified, sitting there on the bed with my blouse halfway off, my breasts exposed and red where this man had rubbed and sucked them. My body was hurting from being pinned under his weight. The memory of his continued rape for what seemed like hours, and masturbating repeatedly on my tiny young body, replayed over and over in my mind. I felt like a piece of dirt.

My parents got home really late that night, after the children were in bed. I was too afraid to tell them what had happened. Being a child, I didn't know how to deal with this hurt and humiliation. Nothing was said about what happened to me—not that night, anyway. After a few days, though, my brother told Mother that this man had been in the bedroom with me for a long time. He went on to tell Mother how he tried hard to get into the room but couldn't because there was something against the door stopping him.

Mother became enraged. She started yelling at me, telling me that I was never going to be anything but a tramp, a whore. I knew I had put up a fight and really tried hard to stop this man from doing these things to me, but Mother made me believe that it was my fault and that I had provoked the rape somehow. For this awful crime I had apparently committed, Mother beat me badly. Over and over she said, "You're nothing but a whore."

This man came back to visit our house many times after that night and was treated like one of the family. I was the dirty one, the whore. I was the one that had made it all happen. I was the one to blame. The dirty drunk man had done no wrong in the eyes of my mother. I'd watch her eyes light up like stars and see that beautiful smile of hers every time he came to visit.

Time moved on as if nothing had happened. On the cold winter nights, Mother would come home after a night on the town, drinking with her friends. The sound of her voice would awaken me in the late hours of the night. The wind howled and the snow crystals were flung into the heavily iced windows at the sides of the small house, making a noise that sounded like a mournful tune. Without opening my eyes, I knew the next day would not be a good one. I snuggled deeper under the thin blanket of the old bed, trying to keep warm.

Morning would come and I would swing my legs over the edge of the bed, intending to ignore the cold chill of the room as I fumbled in the darkness toward the bedroom door. I headed directly to the kitchen, knowing exactly what I'd find: Father standing at the woodstove with a cup of steaming hot tea already in his hand, Mother still in bed sleeping, and the other children standing close to the fire to keep warm as they got dressed for school. Father would make toast. I could see the butter melting in a small dish on the open oven door. With the tips of my fingers I would scratch at the layers of frost on the windows, waiting for the sound of Father's voice telling me to come and get my toast and tea.

Getting my one piece of toast, I felt less important than the family dog. Most days, that was all the food I'd get. Outside, huge drifts of snow piled up against the sides of the house and blocked the path to the water hole, making my walk to fetch the water very hard. With the temperature falling each day, the bitter wind frosted a thick white crust over the top of the snow, making each step even harder. Every night I would pray for spring to come just so I could feel the warm wind in my face and see the water running in the streams. This ray of hope would make my everyday chores much easier. Somehow, those thoughts kept me warm inside. I would shiver as the wind rattled the windows and hope that there would be enough water in the barrel until morning, and that Mother wouldn't send me back to the well for water on such a stormy night.

On most days like that the school would close. We would all be sent home until the storm would pass. As the bus was not picking us up, the walk home was hard. Cutting our own path through the deep snow, we couldn't see two feet in front of us. But I didn't dare stop just putting one foot before the other. I remember thinking as I walked how nice it would be to get home and enjoy a hot bowl of Mother's homemade chicken soup. But as on most days, I would wait for Mother's orders, telling me to come and stand at the family table as they all sat down to eat. My bowl of soup did not look anything like those of the rest of the family. Theirs were full of chicken and vegetables. I was given a bowl of broth. Usually I was told to get away from the table before I was done eating. Mother didn't care if I was hungry or give any thought to how many hours I'd gone without food.

The years passed by slowly. Being a teenager was very frightening. I felt so ashamed because I didn't know anything about starting my period and that it was something that would happen every month. My body was changing. My breasts were growing. The boys were looking at me in a different way that would embarrass me. I didn't like it when they called me Big tits at school.

One week before I started my first period, my teacher had sex education class in school. Just the thought of talking about sex made me feel dirty. All I could think about was the day I got raped and how dirty that man had made me feel. I remembered vividly the pain, the shame, and the embarrassment. My mother's words, "You're nothing but a whore," Echoed in my head all that afternoon. I didn't hear much of anything that my teacher had to say that day.

Mother was outraged when she heard about my teacher talking about sex in class. "That's all I need now," She said, "the likes of you coming home here pregnant."

I didn't even know what the word "pregnant" Meant at that age. I was afraid to let any boy look at me, thinking I might get pregnant. Most of the girls in my class would hang out around the school at night and go to the pool hall to play pool with the guys from school. But I was never allowed to go out at night with my friends. Some nights, Father would send me to the store. I was always so embarrassed to do that because I didn't want my friends to see me carrying the big gas can. But I was happy when father sent me for tobacco because that could fit in my pocket, and no one would have to see it. Those trips to the store would give me some time to hang with my friends and shoot a few games of pool before hurrying back home. Father didn't pay much attention to how long I was gone most of the time because he was busy visiting with his brother, uncle Zack Brown. They would sit for hours each night telling stories.

There was a man at that time who would drive through town in a beautiful, big, dark-coloured car with tinted windows. Sometimes he would stop and give me a ride to and from the store. I would ask him to stop before getting to our house and let me out. I didn't want Mother to find out about him giving me a ride. The first few times he gave me a ride home were okay with me. But then one night he asked me if I wanted to go for a longer ride with him. He said, "Don't worry. I'll have you home before it gets dark, and your mother won't have to know you were in my car."

I got into the car and he drove to Grand Falls. After getting into town, he stopped the car at the ice cream shop and got ice cream for both of us. I thought that was really nice of him. I thanked him for taking me on this ride. When we were done eating, he began to drive us back toward home, but shortly after he drove out of Grand Falls, he made one more stop, at the gravel pit.

I wondered why he was stopping there. It was getting dark. I needed to get home, and I asked him to take me there. "Mother will beat me for this," I told him. He then reached over and pulled me close to him and started to kiss my face.

"I won't hurt you," He said. "I'll take you home in a few minutes. Okay?"

"Okay," I agreed reluctantly. He held me in his arms. I began to feel so special in this man's arms. He whispered words in my ear that I'd never heard before. I felt so wanted for the first time. As the whispered words "I love you!" Reached my ears, I melted in his arms—that night and each night afterward—thinking he would take me away from the horror that was my home.

But how could he do that? I was just eleven years old. Mother would never let me go. I was too young to leave school. This was just a little girl's dream.

But the man promised to always love me and one day to take me away with him forever. I would sit in the back seat of the school bus and watch as he followed on our way to school each day. I couldn't wait for that bus driver to let me off so I could run to the car and let him kiss me before going to class.

Almost every day we were together. Somehow he always took the time to make me feel special. He called me his little girl.

Soon word reached Mother about my being in this man's car. Mother beat me over and over, and I was ordered to never step foot in that car again. But that didn't stop me. I was in love with him. Nothing was going to keep us apart. Mother would have to kill me because I wasn't going to stop seeing him.

Mother kept me in the house for just about six months. The only time I got out after that was for school. No more outings to the store at night. I would look through the windows of our house and cry as he drove by, waving his hand at me.

Finally Father sent me out to the store. I headed down the road. With every step I took, my wish was to see that beautiful car come by and pick me up. It didn't take long. There he was. I got in and off we drove to the gravel pit. I didn't even stop to think about how much trouble I'd be in if Mother found out about us being together. I knew this would end in yet another one of Mother's beatings, but in my mind it was worth it. I told myself it would be just another beating. At this point in my life, what was one more? My mind had learned over the years to turn itself off from pain.

That night Mother sent Father down the road to look for me. When I got home, there she was, waiting with Father standing beside her with the belt in her hand. Within seconds, they were both yelling in my face and saying, "Now get those goddamned clothes off as fast as you can." There I was, at fourteen, standing in front of Father with not a thing on my body.

I couldn't lie my way out of this one because they could see that my breasts were red and swollen from this man touching and rubbing me. When I tried to cover my breasts with my hands, Father pulled them away and hit me in the face, punching me over and over and shouting, "You'll never get in that goddamn car ever again. Will you? Do you hear me?"

I trembled with fear as they both stood there screaming at me. I knew that at any moment they were going to launch into a violent attack for this terrible crime. Father was yelling in my face, "Where were you tonight? And don't tell me you walked up the road because I was up and down that goddamn road, and there wasn't a sign of you anywhere to be seen."

Once again there was no escape. As I stood in front of them, shivering and completely naked, I had no hope of escape. I prayed silently for a miracle. My face felt twice its normal size. Blood rushed to my head as Father threw my body across the floor. There I was with no way out, no choice but to accept what was coming. Father held my body as Mother went on beating me over and over. I begged for her to stop. The more I begged, the harder she hit me. Showing no mercy, she went on and on until she got weak herself.

My fairy-tale dream of a life with this man came to an end in the summer of 1973, not with getting caught but with something else. I was standing at the bus stop a few days after the beating when a girlfriend told me, happily, how in love she was with this same man. She went on to say how he would pick her up and take her for a ride in his nice car. She told me about how her mother didn't like it that she was going with him because he was much older than she was.

"But I love him," She said. That was on a Wednesday afternoon. She was so looking forward to their date on Friday night. I will never forget her last words to me that day: "Sandra, I will die in his arms. Nothing will keep us apart."

Monday morning came and the news was out that she was missing. I felt so sad as I listened to people gossiping that the man in the car had taken her and they had run away together. Police all over the area were on the lookout for them. Roadblocks were put up everywhere to stop them. The news travelled far and wide, and in every town, every eye was open and looking for this evil man who had taken this innocent young girl.

I remember sitting in the back seat of the school bus looking out the window, hoping to see the dark-coloured car behind the bus as I had on previous school days, but it never came. I knew in my heart he would never hurt her in any way.

For some reason my mother and her sister took a drive on tuesday morning through a road where a lot of young people went to park at night. They came upon this man's car parked by the trees. They saw only the back of the car as they pull off to the side of the road. They got out and walked up to the parked car and noticed there was no sound or anything moving inside. Without thinking they both went up to the side of the parked car and looked inside. In the back seat lay the driver of the car, dead, his sightless eyes staring at them. Beside him lay the young lady. She was dead in his arms, just as she had wished to be.

I remember going to the church and seeing two caskets. As I walked up the aisle to say goodbye to my dead friends, I told myself that this was the body of a good man. I thanked him for being so nice to me. I'll love you forever, I whispered.

"I will die in his arms." My friend's words echoed in my mind. My thought at that moment, as I looked down at her body lying in a beautiful casket lined with white satin, was that I wished it was me in that casket and not her. I believe that if I had been allowed out that night, things would not have turned out the way they had.

Time passed quickly. As winter approached, I could imagine the flowers of the field still in bloom as the real ones faded to grey, the trees' autumn beauty now vanished. In a few weeks, everything would be covered with ice and snow. I would sit and wish for summer to return and hoped that it would never end, and it finally did.

During the summer of 1974 my aunt Mae Burt, who lived in corner Brook, had called Mother to ask if one of us girls could come and babysit for her when school opened in September. She knew both my sister and I were good at it, as well as housecleaning and cooking. Aunt Mae was married to my mother's brother. I didn't know them well because they lived three hours away from us, so there wasn't much contact between the two families.

Mother made the plans for me to go. I was happy because that meant getting away from Mother, the name calling, the starvation, and all the beatings. The thought of getting three meals per day made me giddy. I didn't even think about how much money I'd be making, nor did I give any thought to all the shopping I could do when I got paid at the end of the week. That wasn't important at the time. All I could think of was being free from the hands of Mother.

My job was to care for two girls and a boy, do light housework, and make light lunches for when the children got home from school. I remember how beautiful the home was and how clean everything looked. Everything shone. This job was going to be so easy, I thought. They even had a washer and dryer for me to use. I felt like I'd died and gone to heaven. The house was like a dream. My bedroom and the bathroom smelled so clean. I couldn't find dirt anywhere in this beautiful big home.

I was very happy living with and working for this family. They were a family that did things together, and that was very important to them. They were also godly people and went to church every Sunday. Bible reading was very important, and so was praying with the children every night before they went to bed.

My aunt was a very beautiful lady. She was friendly and a great mother. She sewed most of the girls' outfits, and they were so pretty. She was very careful about what the children ate—no junk food was allowed at any time. I remember the first time we had baked chicken at their house. It was the first Sunday I spent with them. My eyes widened as I watched her take all the skin off the chicken and throw it away. I thought to myself: is she crazy? That's the best part, and she's throwing it away!

The first few weeks I was shy. But as time went on, I grew accustomed to this new way of living. I began to feel like a part of the family. For the first time in my life, I felt like I belonged.

After my day's work was done, I would go for a walk, hoping to meet some new friends my own age and maybe hang out with them in the evenings. One night, as I was walking home from a friend's house, singing to myself, out of nowhere came three boys I had never seen before. I knew nothing about them or what they wanted with me. I took a deep breath as they came toward me in the street. Oh my God! I thought. What are they going to do?

It was ten o'clock at night. I was afraid and horrified, not knowing what to do next. I knew those boys were up to no good, just from the way they were looking at me. But there was nowhere to run. I thought maybe they would just talk with me for a while and then leave me alone, but they gathered around me like wild dogs. They started touching my breasts, pushing me, and laughing loudly. They pushed me from one to the other as if I were a human football.

Finally they pulled me into a field and ripped my clothes from my body. I tried to get them off me but failed. Two of the boys had me pinned to the ground. The other one took his pants off and started to masturbate. One by one, they took turns releasing themselves on me as I lay numb on the ground.

I was so cold and shivering with fear. The smell was horrible. After they were finished having their fun, they pulled themselves together and left me alone in the grass. I felt dirty, embarrassed, and so alone. I pulled my body into a fetal position and cried. How could I tell my aunt about this? She would send me back home to Mother. I couldn't let that happen. I didn't ever want to go back home. I decided not to tell anyone about what happened that night. But from that night on I made sure that I was never alone after dark.

My new world fell apart a few months later when my aunt gave me a cheque and told me to buy a bus ticket back home. She didn't need me anymore. I wasn't happy about that at all, so I called up my mother's sister, who lived in the same town, and asked if I could stay with her for a few weeks or until I found a babysitting job. She was very understanding and said, "Yes, Sandra, you can stay here and I'll help you find work."

After a few weeks of living with this second aunt and her family, I went to a little bar just down the street from where we lived to have a game of pool with friends. I overheard a lady talking with her friend about how she was looking for a live-in babysitter, so I told her that I was out of school and looking for a babysitting job. We went on chatting until the bar closed that night. When it was time to leave the bar, Mrs. Rose and her husband gave me a ride to my aunt's house to pick up my things. It was late at night and everyone was sleeping, so I left there without telling my aunt where I was going or who those people were. Without thinking, I just got in the car and drove off with this young couple.

I was to start babysitting that Monday morning. The couple lived out of town in a place called Deer Lake, just outside Corner Brook. After arriving, I found out they had no phone in their little, one-bedroom house. The town was new to me, and I didn't know my way around the streets.

Four days later I took my first walk down to the store to get bread for Mrs. Rose. As I walked around shopping, I noticed the storekeeper looking at me. I thought nothing of it and went on getting the things I needed.

I had just paid for them when I heard a message on the radio saying that anyone knowing the whereabouts of Sandra Brown should call the police. She had last been seen getting into a dark-coloured car at about two o'clock on Sunday morning with two young men.

I thought: What's going on here? What are they talking about? I asked the store manager if there was a pay phone nearby because I needed to call Mother to find out what it was all about. He said, "come on. You can use my office phone to make your call." Within seconds I was talking with Mother. I could tell she was very upset and crying as she talked. In all my life, I'd never heard Mother saying such nice things to me: "Sandra! Are you okay? Did those men hurt you? Where did they take you?" The words that stood out the most were: "come home. Mom loves you!"

Holding back the tears, I wondered what was wrong with her. Why was she talking to me like that? I said: "Mom, slow down and stop crying. I'm fine. I'm working in Deer Lake. What men are you talking about? I'm babysitting for a woman here in Deer Lake." I went on to tell her about the little house where I was now living. "everything is okay," I reassured her. "Don't worry! I'll come home for a visit next weekend," I promised.

"Okay," She said. "Yes." We both said goodbye. I headed back to where I was living and told Mrs. Rose about what was on the news. Just as we were talking, a police car pulled into the driveway. Then two more cruisers appeared. Mrs. Rose went to meet the officers at the door. I was holding the baby in the bedroom. As I looked out the bedroom window, I noticed one of the police officers showing her a picture and asking her if she had seen this young lady. He told her there was a missing persons report on her. "Have you seen her?" He asked again.

Mrs. Rose called me to the door. The police officer asked me my name. I said, "Sandra Brown, sir." He then asked me to step outside. He wanted to talk with me in the police car alone. I said, "Sure, sir." After we got into the car, he said, "I have to bring you back to the police station in Corner Brook for questioning." Once we got to the station, they started to ask me about what took place that night in the bar and how I got to be with those people in Deer Lake. I now realized that things had been taken completely out of context. The story of my being taken by two men that night was not true. I told the police that I called and talked to my mother about this and would be going home on the weekend. The police officer said it was their responsibility to see that I got back home safe with my family. I thought about the irony of that statement.

He looked at me and said, "Do you understand? There is a Canada-wide search out for you, young lady. Your family is sick with worry."

I responded, "I seriously doubt that my mother is sick with worry about me."

Now I was beginning to understand why Mother had been talking to me so sweetly that day on the phone. The house had been filled with people coming and going, wondering if I'd been found yet. Half the town was coming with food or money, helping in any way they could. Mother loved all the attention that this news was bringing her in the little town of Peterview.

Upon my arriving home that night in a police car, there were people everywhere as I walked toward the house. Soon, though,

Mother went back to treating me like a nobody, telling me I would never amount to anything in life. "You'll end up with some old man in a shack somewhere, living on welfare," She threatened.

I thought to myself: No, Mother, you're so wrong about that. Someday I'll be the person you could never be. I'll be a good mother. My children will be proud of me. I won't say anything to make them feel dirty or ashamed. Nor will I give them marks to carry to their grave. And no matter what they do or where they go in life, I'll always be proud of them.

I thank God today for three wonderful children, and for the blessing of becoming a proud grandmother. My children inspired me and kept me going during the stormy years of my life. Also, my beautiful grandchildren are now a very important part of my life. They have given me great joy over the years.

***

Another memory: my sister Ellie and I were outside. We'd picked up bottles and cans and were using them to play with. We put water in the beer bottles for our play party. We were having so much fun together that afternoon, drinking from the beer bottles and telling each other how good the beer was.

Suddenly I heard a tap on the window. I turned to see Mother looking right into my eyes. She gestured to me to come right away. I left my sister and started toward the house. When I got to the bridge, Mother was standing in the doorway, looking at me with that cold look in her eyes. I can still remember that wicked look like it was yesterday. Mother insisted that I get a stick from the wood pile. I knew the stick wasn't to be burned in the woodstove. It was to give me yet another beating for drinking out of the beer bottles. As I was reaching for the stick, the thought went through my mind to run away. But instead I picked up the stick and headed toward the house. Mother was still standing in the doorway, watching as I headed toward her.

Just as I got to the corner of the step, again the thought raced through my mind to run. It was like a voice in my head: "run, run as fast as you can!" I dropped the stick and started to run down the road to nowhere, with no food and just the clothes that I was wearing that day.

I hoped someone would pick me up and help me. As I was running that day I remembered that Mr. Hobbs, a bus driver for the troubled children in our town, would soon be picking up the children to bring them home in his little yellow school bus. Some mornings I would go to his house and wait for his daughter because we were friends and walked to school together. As a little girl I would wish that he was my father. I would stand at the door and watch him as I waited for my friend to get ready for school. He always made sure every one of his children was fed before leaving the house. Their clothes were always picked out the night before and placed on a chair, ready for morning. So I thought when he saw me running scared and far from home, he would stop and pick me up and take me somewhere for help. Again, I didn't understand, as a child, that pain was something felt and not seen.

In the distance behind me, I could hear voices calling my name: "Sandra, stop! Your mother told us to bring you back home. Stop, Sandra! Stop. Wait for us!"

I wasn't about to slow down, never mind stop. I started to run faster, knowing they would catch me at any time.

But all my hard work came to an end when two young men caught up with me and brought me back home to Mother.

Again Mother's rage was out of control. I could hear the boards creaking in the floor each step Mother took as she came after me with a big stick in her hand. Mother asked no questions. She just hit me over and over, yelling, "I'll kill you, you Goddamn Thing. Running away from me like that. I won't leave a bit of you to be seen."

After Mother got done beating me that day, I was ordered to get in that "goddamn room" And make not a sound. She told everyone I was sick in bed. My sister went out to play that day and nothing was said to her, not one word. I sat in the room and wondered why it was so wrong for me to play, and okay for her.

As I walk in the dark of the night To that old water well, I say: Why must they sit warm in the house? Knowing I'm not feeling so well? As I walk along on the cold winter snow, I listen to the wild winds blow. There's a voice that says, "Go, my child, Where your mother wants you to go For the winds will not Take you beneath the deep snow. I've a plan for you. One day, you'll go to a beautiful place Where there is no snow. You'll see much beauty, Much more than one eye can behold, For I am your Heavenly Father. Don't stop! Just go, As I tell you to go. Don't fear the dark nights ... Just go!"

CHAPTER ELEVEN
SWEET SIXTEEN AND PREGNANT

At sixteen I was out of school. I had no job. So I became Mother's slave, doing everything she wanted me to. That included cleaning the house, cooking meals, and raising my younger siblings. There was no end to the work that had to be done.

One day I had cleaned the entire house from top to the bottom. I was working on the floors when my brother came walking through wearing his muddy boots. I asked him to take them off because I'd worked hard to clean the floor. Just as he was taking off his boots, Mother jumped to her feet and told him to go outside and get a stick of wood. "I'll give the likes of you, talking like that around here, telling people to take their boots off. Who in the hell do you think you are?" She yelled in my face.

My brother handed her a long piece of wood, and she started hitting me over and over on my back, head, and legs. There was no stopping her until that stick was in small pieces on the floor. I walked with a limp and pain in my right leg for over a week from the beating I took for no other reason than asking my brother to remove his dirty boots.

I never had the teenage life that most girls my age had. On Saturday nights I would babysit for a family of six children from seven until about three the next morning. I'd get paid just two dollars for the entire night, but I looked forward to it. The children loved me and always wanted me to babysit them whenever their parents went out. I loved and cared for them as if they were my own brothers and sisters. We played board games and card games, cut out pictures from books, sang songs, played church, and watched movies together. They were wonderful children to care for and always so happy. I would always make a special little meal before they went to bed because I didn't want them going to bed hungry.

Mother always had plans for the two dollars that I'd worked so hard for. She'd need milk, bread, or butter. I never got to keep it for myself. It always went to her.

Within weeks of my beginning to babysit for this family, one of the young boys in town started stopping in to visit me. Soon we were boyfriend and girlfriend. He would come to visit after the children went to bed. This had to be a secret. If Mother found out about this, she would stop me from babysitting. I couldn't let that happen because this was my only way to have a little free time away from home.

Time went on and things began to happen between the boy and me. It started with a kiss and him touching my body all over. The first few times I was afraid and pushed him away. I kept thinking about when I was raped and how dirty I felt. But he kept coming back every Saturday night to see me. Soon the touching turned into us having sex. Knowing he cared for me so much and wanted me to be his girlfriend made me feel special. Soon I fell in love with this young man and couldn't picture my life without him.

But once again my happy life and dreams came to an end when Mother looked at me one day and told me to go to the doctor for a checkup. I couldn't understand why she would ask me to do that. But within days I was at the doctor's office. I felt so stupid when he asked me the question, "Now how can I help you, Sandra?"

I didn't know what to say to him. I told him my mother told me to come for a checkup, and that was all.

He then asked me if I was having pain anywhere in my body.

I answered, "No, doctor. Not at all."

Then he asked, "are you still having your headaches?"

I said, "No, doctor. They haven't been giving me too much trouble in the past few months."

He then surprised me by asking me, "are you pregnant, Sandra?"

I was scared. I had a sick feeling in my stomach. I looked at him and said honestly, "I don't know."

Then he gave me a bottle and asked me to go in the washroom and pee in the bottle. I took the test. In just a few days, the results came back. I was going to have a baby.

I remember being so afraid of what Mother was going to do when she found out that I was pregnant. I was afraid she would beat me. So I kept it from her as long as I could.

Months passed. I was starting to show and having morning sickness. Finally, Mother asked, "are you pregnant, Sandra?"

In a low, soft voice I said, "Yes, Mom. I'm pregnant."

Predictably, she started to yell. "Now you made your bed. You can lie in it. You will stay in this house and look after that baby when it comes."

"Okay, Mom," I said. I went back to doing my work, cleaning the house.

Later that night, Mother demanded that I tell her the name of the baby's father. After I told her, she ordered me not to see him again. Mother's orders not to see this young man upset me very much because we really wanted to be together. I was sure if he knew he was going to be a father, he would want to do the right thing. He would want to be married before the baby was born.

With those thoughts in my mind, I couldn't wait to tell him the good news. One night I got out for a few hours, so I got together with him and told him that we were going to have a baby. In the beginning he seemed very happy with the news, but eventually I realized he didn't want anything to do with me or the baby. Night after night I would sit in the old armchair, looking out the window.

I'd watch in misery as he drove up and down the road with girls in his car, as if I didn't even exist anymore.

Mother would watch me cry because I was so upset over the way this guy was treating me. Every night Mother got dressed up and went out on the town like a teenager. She'd look at me in passing and say, "Now shut up. It's no good to cry now. You didn't think he was going to stay with the likes of you, did you?" I just wanted her gone. I didn't care if she got killed in the street. I wished every night that she was out that I would never have to see her or hear that voice of hers ever again as long as I lived.

One night the baby's father came to visit. He wanted to ask Father if he could marry me and do things right before the baby was born. But Father told him to wait and ask my mother. He didn't want to have any say in the matter. So we waited to get Mother on a day when she was in a good mood, thinking that would make a difference. Maybe she would be happy that we wanted to do what was best for the baby.

But Mother became enraged with us. She told him to get out of the house and never come back again. She warned him that if he ever came back, she would call the police and have him locked up in jail.

The boy and I talked about waiting until I turned eighteen. We both knew there was nothing Mother could do to stop us at that age. But it was not to be.

On September 9, 1975, I checked into the Grand Falls Hospital to have surgery for an abscess inside my breast. The surgery went well but it was a long road to recovery due to all the infection that had built up over the weeks leading up to it. By September 13, still in hospital, I started to feel pressure and found it hard to sit on a chair. I spent most of that day in my bed, tossing and turning with my breast wrapped in tight binding. I was given nothing for pain because it might harm the baby.

The next morning I woke up feeling a little better, so I got out of bed. Throughout the day I walked the hallway a few times. As evening came, the pressure was coming back, a little heavier this time. I didn't know what was going on and didn't say anything to the nurses.

I got back in my bed and again tossed and turned through the night. It felt like I had to urinate, but every time I went to the bathroom to pee I couldn't. This going in and out of the bathroom and not being able to pee went on for a few hours.

I was in a room with three other older ladies. One of them asked me if I was having pain. I said, "Just in my breast." She then asked if I was in labour.

I said, "No, it feels like I have to pee, that's all."

She said, "I'm going to ring my bell for the nurse to come and see you."

I turned back on my side and tried to rest. Soon the nurse came and I was taken to the maternity ward where the doctor on call that night gave me a pelvic examination. After he was done, he said, "Young lady, you're going to be a mommy real soon."

The nurses got me ready to deliver my baby. I was so afraid, not knowing what was going to take place. The pain was coming and going. I kept saying, "That's not too bad." The nurses reminded me that it was going to get a lot harder before it was over.

The pain kept up all through the night and into morning, but the baby was not coming. I was getting very hot. The nurse opened the windows so I could feel the cool breeze coming in, but even that wasn't much help. As the hours passed the pain grew much worse. I got really scared when the nurses started to run for the doctor to come and check on me every few minutes.

Every time I saw the doctor coming toward my bed and putting on those white surgical gloves as he walked, I would cry, "Oh my, not again! It hurts so much. Please just leave me alone."

Finally, the doctor said, "We're going to have to do surgery." He then asked the nurse to call my mother to come and sign the paperwork giving them permission to do surgery as I was still a minor. I remember how the nurse went running to make the call, but they couldn't reach Mother. The pains were getting harder and longer each time they came. My breathing had become laboured.

The doctor came back into the room and gave the order to have me taken down to the Or. He told me they couldn't wait for my mother. They were now working hard to save me and my baby.

Within seconds they put the mask on my face and told me to count backwards from ten to one. I was now counting and thinking, God, if the baby doesn't make it, take me too. That was my last thought before going into a deep sleep that day.

I awakened to the sound of a nurse saying, "Sandra, you have a beautiful baby girl."

With tears in my eyes, I asked, "Is she okay?"

The nurse said, "Your baby is gorgeous, with beautiful blue eyes and rosy cheeks."

***

I wasn't afraid of being a mother. I'd worked hard to help my older sister raise my young siblings. Once I fully recovered from both surgeries, my baby and I went home to live with the family.

Shortly after I got home, Mother took me to apply for welfare. Mother did most of the talking because I was too young, she said, and wouldn't understand the questions they would be asking. I signed my name to all the paperwork, not really knowing what I was doing.

After that was done, I started receiving a cheque at the end of every month to feed myself and the baby. I remember how nice Mother would treat me just a few days before the cheque came in the mail each month and how happy she was to go shopping.

Mother was always the one to take me shopping with a big smile on her face, as if she'd decided it would be Sandra's special day. She would take the shopping cart and fill it with food as if it were her money. "Now pick up the baby's milk," She would say in a sweet voice. After the sales clerk checked everything through the cash, I sign my cheque and pass it over. Once the food was paid for, there was very little money left to do anything with.

But it was very important to me that I had a special treat to give my daughter because she liked them so much. I remember one time I had candies in my dresser drawer. I was saving them to give her one every day because it would be a long time before I got my next cheque. As I went to get a candy for my daughter one day, I found they were gone. I took everything out of the dresser looking for them but found nothing. I got so upset that I started to ask my younger sisters and my baby brother if they had taken the candy. Right away they started crying and saying, "Mom, Sandra is saying we took the candy, but we didn't."

Mother got all crazy and started yelling at me. "I'll give the likes of you, saying they took the candy," She threatened.

I retorted, "Well, the candy didn't just walk away."

It was the wrong thing for me to say. Mother took the broom and came after me. "I'll kill you, you Goddamn Thing!" She yelled. She kept hitting me until that broom handle was broken in pieces. I felt so sad to hear my daughter crying, "Mommy! Mommy!" It scared her to watch her mommy get beaten like that. With my back aching, I reached down and picked her up. I held her tightly in my arms to make her feel safe and to let her know her mother was okay.

I wanted to kill my mother that day, but not for what she had done to me. The thought of her scaring my baby like that made me want to rip her head off.

"What were you thinking?" I said to her as I held my daughter. "are you out of your fucking mind? To do that around the baby?" I was no longer afraid of Mother and wasn't about to let her get away with her sick games anymore. My baby was not going to be a victim of Mother's outrage. There was no way I was going to let that happen.

I was counting down the days to my eighteenth birthday so I could be out of Mother's house, married, and on my own. But the days until then seemed to have no ending. Mother was still in control of my life, taking my money, telling me when to come and go. Her words rang in my ears over and over. "You'll never be any-thing but a whore!" She'd scream. "You'll end up with a house full of babies and no one to help take care of them. You're so stupid no man will ever stay with the likes of you!"

By the time I was seventeen Mother's words were planted deep in my head. Part of me believed every word she said. I hoped and prayed to get out of that house before my daughter was old enough to understand the words that were coming out of her grandmother's mouth.

My childhood beatings and neglect continued. Now, being a young mother myself, they made me embarrassed and ashamed of still being subjected to abuse. I kept telling myself to be strong. I felt that, as long as I had my baby to care for, I could handle any situation that Mother threw my way. I stayed at home to help raise my daughter and the younger siblings.

Mother was gone most of the time. She wouldn't get home until two or three in the morning. Before she would finally get home from wherever she was night after night, the other children in the house and I would watch Father pace from window to window, wondering where she was. Father loved and cared for Mother so much. Every stormy night in winter he would shovel the walkway to make sure it was safe for when Mother got home.

Some nights he would ask her where she was coming from so late. "I've been walking the floor wondering where you were," He'd complain tentatively, reluctant to upset her.

Mother would become outraged with him, just because he was concerned about her well-being. She would start yelling at Father and saying, "Where in the hell do you think I was?" Sometimes she would throw things around the house. Mother didn't care about anyone but herself. She gave no thought to the babies in the room, who might get hit in the crossfire. She'd toss things around like a madwoman out of control. There was no stopping her. Father would run from Mother, but the children had nowhere to turn. We were stuck in the middle of Mother's tantrum.

At seventeen I was still, in many ways, afraid of Mother. There were times I would lock myself and the baby in my bedroom to get away and feel safe from Mother as she would go on yelling at the top of her voice. I remember crying and making almost no sound. I didn't want my daughter to see that I was afraid of Mother. I wanted her to feel safe in my arms. I held her tight and rocked her to sleep each night and sang beautiful, soft, baby song in her ears. I knew in my heart this little girl was my life. I had to be strong and keep her safe.

I couldn't afford to give my little girl the things I wanted her to have. We got by on very little money, but I made sure she didn't go hungry or cold and showered her with all the love I could give. I would dress her up in pretty dresses and matching bows in her hair. I would go walking up and down the road with her just to show her off and let people see how beautiful she was. Some people would pull their cars over to the side of the road and have a little talk to her and say, "What a sweet little girl you are!" They would say, "She looks like a walking doll."

I remember smiling at those compliments. I felt so proud of her. This beautiful little blue-eyed girl was my daughter charlene. For the first time in my life, I had been given a wonderful gift that was all mine. No one was going to take her away from me, not even my mother with all her controlling power. My baby was not going to be Mother's victim.

CHAPTER TWELVE

MY ESCAPE

In February 1977 Mother was in the hospital with high blood pressure. Father and I took care of the children at home, as on every other day. The only thing different this time was that Mother was in the hospital. Did the family worry about her well-being? Yes. After all, she was the mother in the home. But it gave us great peace and serenity not having to tolerate her nasty behaviour, even if it was only for a few days. Everything felt normal when Mother was away.

My older sister, Patty, was now living in Toronto. She called home every Sunday to check on how the family was doing. I told my sister Mother was in the hospital again with high blood pressure and let her know there was no reason to be worried. We got to talking about how things were at home and how Mother was still in control of my life, taking all the money and leaving me with nothing. There was no way I could make changes for myself and my baby without money.

My sister and I came up with an escape plan for me to get away from home and Mother's violent attacks. She promised to call back that night and tell Father she had a job in Toronto waiting for me. Father would talk to Mother about this job plan the next time he went to visit her at the hospital, and I wouldn't have to deal with Mother after she came home from the hospital. My sister made the flight plans. Mother was to let me keep my money at the end of the month to pay for my flight.

I was happy to finally pack what little I owned and take my daughter to Toronto for what I hoped would be a better life. I was elated to leave the anguish of my past behind me. On February 22, 1977, I left home with no thought of ever returning. Sitting on the plane that day, I remember talking to my little girl about how beautiful life would be in Toronto, though I knew she was too young to understand what I was talking about. How could she? She was just two years old at the time.

As the plane started descending toward Toronto, I saw the city lights for the first time. It was thrilling and scary at the same time. I knew I was on my way to a new life, but I didn't know what that new life was going to be all about.

My sister met us at the airport and drove us to her apartment. Everything was so homey looking, so beautiful, and I felt free for the first time in my life. I lived with my sister for my first six months in Toronto. There was no job waiting. That was just a lie that my sister made up as part of the plan to get me away from Mother.

I went to social services for help, and they set me up on a mother's allowance. Again the paperwork was done. I signed my name to get money at the end of every month. But this time it was different. Finally I was in control of making plans and shopping with my own money. I felt as free as a bird in the sky—free to fly!

After months of staying with my sister, I went to visit an old school friend who now lived on the lakeshore. I loved the view of the lake because it reminded me of Newfoundland.

The one part of home I missed the most was the ocean. This was where we were going to live, I decided, as we walked along the lakeshore streets. It would be another new beginning. This would be our first time living on our own—though the prospect of that was a little overwhelming.

My friend helped me to get an apartment on Sixth Street in that neighbourhood. This place was just a little basement apartment with no bedroom. It had a bathroom with a bathtub and shower, hot and cold running water, and a small kitchen with a stove. The bigger room had a tv. I added a sofa bed that I could pull out at night for my daughter and me to sleep on.

My support cheque for the month was two hundred and ninety-eight dollars at that time. My monthly rent was one hundred and sixty dollars, so it didn't leave us much to live on.

My friend Karen and I would take the streetcar all the way to downtown Toronto, to a place called the Scott Mission. They had a food bank, a place to go once a month to get free food. They didn't give you much, but any food at all was a big help. I was given ten bus tokens per month to take the bus or streetcar. Karen and I would get started early in the morning and wouldn't get back until late in the evening.

Karen was from Toronto, born and raised. She was always finding ways to give me a helping hand and showing me how to get the most out of my money. Karen and her family became my lifetime friends. She was a wonderful cook, and my daughter and I would eat with them often. Karen, her husband, Stanley, and their two girls became like family to us. Charlene, Cindy, and Jen played and got along well together.

The first few months of being on my own were good. But then I began to feel the pressure of raising my little girl alone without much money. I remember the last week of every month I would go hungry because there was only enough food to feed my daughter. Old memories started to get me down and I became depressed. I began looking for another kind of escape. That escape came in the form of a new group of friends and a world I'd never seen before: parties, drugs, and alcohol.

The nightclubs and my new-found friends seemed to bring relief for a while, but soon I found myself getting in too deep. This life had me caught in a trap. I pulled back from it, and the people I thought were my friends soon forgot about me. Once more I found myself alone. No one seemed to care if I was dead or alive.

I felt like I was starving for love and attention. Soon I met someone who seemed to be everything I was looking for. Wayne showered me with gifts. We were eating takeout food just about every day of the week. Wayne really seemed to care about the well-being of my daughter. He paid for weekend babysitters so we could go out drinking and dancing with friends. We had the world by the tail. It seemed every day was a new experience.

Little by little we got more involved in the night life. Wayne introduced me to his friends. Night after night the crowd got bigger. They'd arrive on Harleys and other bikes of all colours and sizes. Weekends became all about money, drugs, and alcohol, and we regularly took weekend road trips to the north of Toronto.

We were living on top of the world, drinking and doing hard drugs. There was no end to the parties. Many nights we would get stoned out of our minds. For kicks and a little fun we would cruise the city streets. We'd do a little bar-hopping and cause some kind of disturbance that would lead to being arrested by the city police. At this point the life of the biker gang seemed to me to have it all. They just didn't care about anyone or anything but themselves.

We were now a part of the biker family. I knew that as long as they were in my life, no harm would ever come to me or my daughter. We had each other's backs, no matter what. My new family looked out for my daughter and me. I dressed her in little Black biker boots, a Black leather vest, blue jeans, and a headband. Some of the biker girls would take her in their sidecars to ride with them. They loved showing her off everywhere we went.

One of the few days I was sober, I remember thinking of my little girl and what a crazy world I was trying to raise her in. One day in particular that stands out in my mind was the day Wayne was teaching charlene how to eat chicken. "Do it like a biker," He said, going on to show her how to rip it apart and stuff her little mouth full. As I stood there watching the chicken juice run down her chin, I thought, God, she looks like a little animal. Wayne and the other bikers thought it was really cute and laughed about it. Wayne looked at one of his buddies and said, "She'll make a fine Biker Brood one day."

I knew I had to stop this crazy way of living. I needed to give my daughter a better life than this. I tried to reason with Wayne and let him know how I felt. But then I was faced with threats of violence and even death if I tried to leave him. One time I told him I was taking my daughter and leaving, and there was nothing he could do to stop me. He took me by the throat and started to push his knife into my chin. He applied enough pressure to bring blood. He said, "You're my woman. No woman leaves me without paying the price."

There it was again. All that old fear came bubbling back to the surface. I never told him again that I wanted out. I stayed there like his prisoner, doing whatever he wanted me to. But I never gave up hope of getting out. Without a word to anyone, I was making plans in my head to get away.

We went on road trips every weekend, drinking and doing hard drugs. This was now my way of life. Each night I was in a bar fight with someone—man or woman, it didn't matter to me. Things were getting out of control. There was no easy way out. Night after night I would cry, "God, this is not the life I want to live. Please help me find a way out before I get myself killed."

One night we were at the eastwood Hotel on the lakeshore. I'd been drinking for two days without sleep. At last call, some guy said something to me that I didn't like. I threw my drink in his face and told him to shut the fuck up and leave me alone. As I watched him come at me, I got myself ready for one hell of a fight. Tables and drinking glasses flew everywhere. The whole bar joined in. The police were called. I thought: This is my night to run. And run I did. But being so drunk, I didn't get far—just a few blocks down the street.

Two rough-looking guys put me in a white van and drove off to an open field, where they pulled me out, pushed my body to the ground and put a knife to my throat. The bigger guy said, "You're not going anywhere, bitch." Within

Seconds they were taking turns raping and beating me over and over. In the field that night I could hear the sound of the van as they drove away, leaving my helpless body behind for dead. Everything went Black. I don't remember anything else about that night or how many days and nights went by before my body was found.

When I opened my eyes, there were two biker girls cleaning me up. I tried to move but couldn't. My body had taken a bad beating and was still very weak. I knew at this point there was nowhere to run.

The more Wayne beat me, the more I would drink to kill the pain. But in November 1978 freedom came at last, in the least expected manner. A few months after my body had been found in the field, badly beaten, Wayne had left the apartment, telling me to get a babysitter because we were going on the road for a few days. I was to get ready because he would be coming to pick me up at five that evening to leave for our road trip. Five o'clock came and went. Then six. The night went on. No Wayne. I was beginning to think that he wasn't coming back at all. He didn't show up at all that night, and I don't know if I was glad that he was gone or just scared. By this time Wayne's kind of life was all I knew.

I didn't hear anything from him for about a month. Then one of his friends got out of jail and told me that he'd seen Wayne there. He'd been arrested for armed robbery about a month ago and would be doing five years in the Don Jail. I remember looking up into the sky that day and saying, "Thank you, Jesus!" I knew in my heart it was the work of God. Once again I'd been set free.

The next few months, I got busy trying to clean my life up and get free from the drugs and alcohol that were in my body. I had a fight on my hands. Getting clean wasn't an easy thing to do. I was sick every other day as my body went through withdrawal.

I tried hard to spend my time with my daughter, taking her for long walks. Without much money to do things, most days, walking and going to the parks was all we did. We'd watch the light snow fall on the ground as we sat on the old park bench, feeding the birds. Each night we watched the sun go down together, thankful to be free of the biker life.

CHAPTER THIRTEEN

THE FIGHT TO GET MY DAUGHTER BACK

I settled into a new apartment and devoted all my time to my little girl. I took her on bus rides and to parks, playgrounds and restaurants, trying hard to make up for lost time. I wanted to give my daughter everything I'd missed out on in life as a child. Nothing was too much when it came to my daughter.

One day I received a phone call from my sister Patty. She told me she was going to move back home to live in Newfoundland. At that time my sister was my only friend. I felt as if the bottom had dropped out of my world, but I continued to give it my best shot. I tried to put all my energy into raising my daughter. The biker world was now just a bad memory. Unfortunately so was all the money, fast food, and easy living. We were now on our own with just enough money to pay rent on our new one-bedroom apartment on 43rd Street. This new place was much bigger and brighter. We loved living there because it was across the street from Mary curtis Park.

With my sister gone back to Newfoundland, my life seemed empty. Charlene and I had really looked forward to the weekend visits at Patty's house. Charlene had loved spending time there because she and her cousin Jason were close in age and played well together. My sister had always made sure that we had food to take home with us, and that food had been a big help.

One night I was sitting alone in my apartment, feeling very depressed, and charlene began to cry. I tried everything I could think of to get her to stop: walking the floor with her, singing to her, and rocking her in my arms. But she kept crying. I thought I'd take her out to get some french fries because that was her favourite food. But when we came back home, she wouldn't eat them. She just screamed harder and louder.

By this time I was at my wits' end. "What are you crying about?" I yelled in her face. "I can't take this anymore," I warned her. "It's been going on for most of the day. What's wrong with you? Stop your crying and tell me what is wrong, so I can help make things better for you." I was going to lose my mind if she didn't stop this crying soon. I remember the cat jumping up on the table. I hated that Black cat. It looked at me that night with its eyes shining as if it were ready to come at me at any moment.

I screamed at the cat insanely: "Get off the table! Get down! I'll fucking kill you. Get off the fucking table!" But the cat just curled up in a ball and sat there on the table as if it didn't even hear me. "That's it!" I shouted. "I've had enough of this fucking bullshit for one night!" I jumped up and ran toward the cat saying, "I'll kill the likes of you and won't leave a bit of you to be seen!"

Charlene was crying and screaming, "No, Mommy, no! Don't hurt my cat!" She loved the cat so much. I just wanted to kill it that night. I was so out of control. I threw the table and chairs across the house, hitting the cat. The damned cat flew across the living room, into the bedroom and under the bed. Still yelling at the top of my voice, I screeched, "If you come out here anymore this goddamn night I'll fucking kill you!"

The cat was out of the way. Now I was screaming at my daughter, saying things I didn't even realize I was saying. Before I knew what was happening, I began to hit her over and over with my hand. My mother's words just poured from my mouth. I kept yelling in her face and saying, "I'll kill you! I won't leave enough of you to be seen!"

It seemed as if I'd lost all control of myself. My mother had taken over my body. I struggled and tried to get a grip. Then, all of a sudden, I heard a loud knock at my door. I tried to pull myself together before opening it. The knocking grew even louder.

When I opened the door, two police officers were standing there, staring at me. One of them stepped forward and asked me if I was upset. They had received a phone call from someone in the building complaining about the noise coming from my apartment. I just stood at the door and stared at them, speechless. Then I burst into tears. As one of the officers was trying to calm me down, the other one went into my bedroom. Before I realized what was going on, he had the bedroom completely stripped as they were searching for drugs.

He asked me if I'd been doing drugs or drinking. I shook my head no. Then both officers went over to the sofa to talk with my daughter. They saw the print of my hand on her leg. I noticed one of the officers making a call to someone. Within twenty to thirty minutes of his making the call, a man dressed in a suit and tie arrived.

I couldn't figure out what was going on. Who is this man? I'd never seen him before in my life. Without saying a word, he went over, picked my daughter up in his arms, and walked toward the door. I asked the officers, "What is going on with this man? Who is he? Why is he walking out the door with my daughter in his arms?" They told me my daughter was in good hands, and they were going to take her for the weekend. The officer then suggested that I go to the hospital and talk with a doctor about what was troubling me.

The man who walked off with my daughter in his arms was a family services officer responsible for child welfare. The memory of my daughter's face and her baby voice crying out for me as this man walked away with her on that cold November night will always remain with me. After they left my apartment, I couldn't think of anything except the fact that, just like that, my daughter was gone. I wasn't anywhere near capable of thinking anything out clearly. I refused to leave my apartment and go see a doctor.

All weekend I stayed home and sat on the sofa where my daughter had been lying when they took her away. I cried the whole weekend.

Monday finally came. I walked the streets and found a phone booth to call the Department of Social Services to explain what had happened on Friday night. I wanted to know when they would be bringing Charlene back home to me. The lady I was talking with said, "Miss Brown, someone will be coming by to visit with you today."

I went back home and calmly awaited the visit from the children's aid worker. When she arrived she wanted me to explain why I'd been so upset. I couldn't think of anything to say except that I'd had a bad night. She told me they would be keeping charlene in their care until they were sure I wouldn't hurt her anymore. She went on to tell me to find a lawyer and get some help from a psychiatrist. She said I needed to be calm and relaxed.

My mind was in turmoil. I just kept thinking: How in hell could I be calm and relaxed when they had my daughter? Charlene was the only thing I had in this world. Now they were telling me they were going to keep her. I didn't know at this point whether I'd ever see her again.

I asked myself how it could be happening. It was like a nightmare with no ending. And they wanted me to stay calm? When the children's aid worker left that day, I was completely alone. The next few days I tried everything I could think of to get my daughter back home with me again.

My last hope was my mother. I called her from a pay phone, praying that she'd be of some help, that she'd tell me what to do or where to turn next. She just went on yelling in my ear saying, "You're nothing but a tramp on the streets! You don't deserve to have a child." My only hope for help was crushed. Now I knew I was totally alone with my problem. My hands got weak and I dropped the phone. I did nothing but cry as I slowly walked back home without hope of ever seeing my little girl again.

I sat around the apartment and prayed, "God, keep charlene safe and somehow let her know her mommy loves her." I prayed the same prayer every night as I sat and watched the time pass, minute by minute. Time and faith in God were all I had left.

Soon I was back in the bars, drinking as much as I could, because getting drunk helped me forget the pain of losing my daughter. I was now drinking steadily each day, from the moment I opened my eyes in the morning until I passed out drunk at night. Sometimes I'd wake up in the hospital not even knowing how I'd gotten there. I had no memory of where I'd been the night before. I drank anything I could get my hands on, and getting a drink was easy in those days. In the late 1970s and early 1980s, all I had to do was walk into a bar wearing a low-cut top, tight blue jeans, and a smile, and men would be all over me like wild dogs. Within seconds, someone was passing me a drink.

Many nights after the bar closed, I'd leave and walk the streets of Toronto, hoping to find my way home. Night after night the police would stop and pick my drunk body off the sidewalk and put me in the drunk tank at the Don Jail to sober up. The hours in a small cell didn't matter much to me. I had nothing and no one to go home to. The police would eventually release me and give me a bus ticket to get home. But the drinking didn't stop. In fact, it got much worse. Every day and every night I'd be either drunk or stoned out of my mind on drugs.

Two weeks after my daughter was taken from me, I received another visit from the children's aid worker. It was a man this time. He told me he had received a phone call from my family in Newfoundland. My mother wanted Charlene placed in her care. I felt as if he'd punched me in the stomach. I couldn't breathe, and my mind was reeling. I began to kick the table leg and scream, telling him he was crazy. I'd never let that woman take my little girl.

"I don't care if I never see her again," I told him. "My mother is not to have anything to do with raising my daughter. Do you hear me?" Then I begged him, "Please don't let that happen. My mother is not going to do to my daughter the things that she did to me as a little girl. Please!" I begged. "Charlene is not to go to Newfoundland with my mother."

By this time I was out of control. I just cried and cried as he sat there staring into my eyes. When I'd calmed down enough for him to speak, he said, "Miss Brown, I understand now. Please don't feel badly about what happened. Just see someone and explain to them what your childhood was like." He gave me phone numbers of people to call for help, and I agreed to use them. I had finally reached rock bottom. The mere thought of my wonderful Charlene being subjected to what I'd had to endure with my mother was the wake-up call I needed.

From that day forward things started to look up for me again. I set up a meeting with my psychiatrist and talked to her about my childhood pain. I told her about the hurt that I had carried around for years. Miraculously, talking about it seemed to heal me. Getting some of it out in the open was helping me to start letting it go. I realized that I was no longer alone. My next step toward getting Charlene back would be to stop drinking and get off the drugs. I finally had the help I needed. All I had to do was reach out and take the free help that was waiting. For the next few weeks I was busy in meetings every day, doing whatever it took to win this fight for my daughter. I was beginning to sound like a broken record, telling my story over and over to people I'd never seen before in my life.

I also found a lawyer, and it wasn't long before I was in court petitioning to get my daughter back. As I sat in the courtroom that morning, it seemed like the hearing was taking forever. I don't remember everything that was said there, but I'll always remember the judge's words, "The child will be placed back home with her mother." Those words were like magic to me. I was being given a second chance. My baby would be coming home. Elated and with big tears in my eyes, I looked up at the judge and said, "Thank you, sir!" The judge went on to say he believed that "Miss Sandra Brown has her problems under control, and from now on if she's in need of help, there are people she can call to talk with." I left the court-house that day with this thought in my mind: Thank you, God, for this day! I'll never let her go again.

April 11, 1979, was one of the most important days in my life. Charlene was home for easter Sunday, just as I'd wished. As Charlene opened her easter gifts, my eyes filled with tears. She looked up at me with the most beautiful smile on her face and said, "Mommy, I love you." I dropped the things that were in my hands, took her in my arms, and said, "Thank you, baby. Mommy is never letting you go again."

Time sped by. We lived each day like it was our last. I wasn't about to take one day with her for granted.

A few months prior to getting my daughter back home, I had met a young man who became my rock. Ambrose had supported me in my decision to get my little girl back, and for a while we were happy. He was a kind man with a steady job and a loving family. I gave birth to a beautiful new baby girl, Hannah, on August 31, 1979.

A new baby girl! Our little family was complete. We were very happy together for about three years. Then our lives took us down different roads. Ambrose and I ended our relationship in 1981, but we remain friends to this day. I will always be thank-ful to Ambrose Downey for being a rock at that time in my life. I was now strong and ready to move on with my two daughters, Charlene and Hannah.

Once again I turned to my good friend Karen. I made arrange-ments to stay with her and her family until I got enough money together for my own place. With open arms Karen and her family welcomed us into their home.

During the next few months I worked hard and put in long hours to save money for a new apartment. My job was cleaning motel rooms. I would clean twenty-five rooms, five days a week. I made four dollars and fifty cents per hour, and the work was hard. With only a grade three education, I was unable to find a good-paying job. But when it came to cleaning and making beds, that was something I was really good at. I didn't need to read or write to get the job.

CHAPTER FOURTEEN

SECRETS

As a child, my dream was to grow up and find a man who would love and care for his family, protect us, and be there through good and bad times. In 1981 I was now living back in Newfoundland and I believed I had found this man. We were married in February 1982. For the first time in my life, I felt happy and loved.

In May 1982 we welcomed a new baby boy, Curt Douglas, into our family. I could not have been happier. But in just ten years my world would come crashing down once again. On May 29, 1992, I awakened to the sound of the telephone ringing. The sun was shining brightly through my bedroom window. My husband was sleeping peacefully beside me. It was the social worker from Grand Falls who had been working with my younger daughter, Hannah since April. She asked me if it would be okay for her to come to my house to speak with me. I invited her over. When she arrived, she asked if my husband was at home. I said, "Yes, he's here." Then she asked me if I'd go out for coffee with her because she really needed to talk to me alone.

We were both very concerned about my daughter, who had attempted suicide. I couldn't understand why my little girl would want to die. My world fell apart as I learned that the man who had promised to care for our family turned out to be my children's worst nightmare.

Soon I was sitting in a meeting with the social worker, corporal Nippard from the RCMP office in Grand Falls, and my daughter. We sat quietly as Corporal Nippard questioned my daughter about what was troubling her. I sat trembling, staring at her as I listened to the words that came from her young mouth. I watched the tears roll down her cheeks. I couldn't sit in that room any longer. I had to leave. I knew then that I had to make a decision that would protect my little girl. I had to keep her safe, safe from the one person aside from me that I thought would always protect and shelter her. I had to rescue her from my husband.

I didn't think I would ever hear anything worse than what my child had to say that morning. But that same afternoon my heart was torn again when I was told that this man, who I had thought would make all my dreams come true, had confessed to sexually molesting my oldest daughter Charlene, who was now living in Toronto.

Finally I understood why my little girl wanted to kill herself. The man she called Daddy had terrible secrets. I made a decision that day to protect my children, to keep them safe and free from fear. But inside I was torn. I knew my girls needed me to be strong for them. On the other hand I had to consider my son, a nine-year-old boy who loved his daddy very much and couldn't understand why he was no longer allowed to live in our home.

My heart broke as my little son looked at me with big tears streaming down his face. The only thing I could tell him was that Daddy had done something wrong, and so he couldn't stay with us anymore. I knew he could never understand the real reason. I watched him go into his room, sit on the bed, and cry over the family pictures for hours. I tried to comfort him and tell him that everything would be okay and that he'd see his dad again soon, but I wasn't even sure if I believed that myself. What mattered most at that time was doing and saying the right things around my son. His world had been torn apart.

My husband was tried and convicted of sexual assault against my older daughter in the summer of 1992. I packed up what little I owned and the two children, Hannah and Curt Douglas, and moved to Salisbury, New Brunswick, to live with my friend Gwen and her family. We hoped we'd be able to make a new start. We tried to leave the unhappy past behind us, with the help of good friends and public assistance. Although I was relieved to be away from Newfoundland, where I had endured such pain for so many years, I discovered that you can't escape the past. The past came back to haunt us.

My children had a lot of built-up anger and resentment, and although counselling helped, it didn't make the pain disappear. My son, especially, was deeply affected by the breakup of our marriage. He was hurt and resentful about not being able to see his dad. As he grew older, things got out of control. I reached out for help for myself and my son. With my own history of being abused by my mother, I was afraid I might lose my patience and do something to hurt him. So I agreed that it would be better for my son if I placed him in foster care. I kept in close contact with my son and his caretakers. My heart was breaking to have to let him go. This was yet another tough decision I had to make to protect one of my children.

I knew that keeping my husband's secret was wrong, and I had to deal with it somehow. I was not about to hide forever the thing that had torn my children's world apart. Unlike everyone else, I was not going to cover up my husband's crime. If I did, then I would be no better than my husband and my mother. I believed that dark secrets from their own past lives had made my mother and my husband the way they were. Things do happen for a reason. I wanted to know what had caused them to behave the way they had done because I didn't want the pattern to be repeated in the next generation. I didn't want my children to come from the same kind of world as I had done. These problems would not go away by hiding them in the back of my mind, as if everything was fine. I decided it was time to take a stand.

My mother's words still pounded in my head from when I was a little girl. I remembered her shouting at me, "You'll never be anything. No man will ever want anything to do with you. You'll just live in dirt with a house full of kids, raising them on your own."

I was not about to let Mother continue controlling my life. I cursed her and said to myself that she would eat her words one day. I tried to compose myself. Screwing up was the last thing I could allow to happen. I loved my children and wanted the best for them. I realized that some of the choices I had made as a mother hadn't always been the best. I will have to live for the rest of my life regretting some of my actions.

I prayed one day my son would come to understand that I had made my choices for him for all the right reasons. Sometimes it's hard for a child to understand what a mother will do to keep her children safe, just as a baby bird doesn't understand why its mother pushes it out of the nest, knowing it has never flown before. But I thought: Soon the storm will pass and you'll understand why, my son. You'll learn that your mother needed help to learn how to fly.

CHAPTER FIFTEEN

HAUNTING MEMORIES

Violence has always been a big part of my life, it seems, and often I'd find myself expressing my anger in abusive ways. When I would go out on the weekends for drinks with friends, I'd usually get into a fight with someone. As time went on, the fights got more violent. Coming home with my face badly cut and bruised, for days I would stay in my bedroom and wouldn't come out. I would lie to my children and tell them I'd hurt myself falling down the stairs. It was the best excuse I could think of.

My husband tried everything in his power to help me. He'd say, "Sandra, you're taking your anger out on the wrong people. These people you're picking fights with aren't doing anything to hurt you. It's your parents that did you wrong all those years ago. You need to get help with anger management before someone presses charges and you end up in jail." I knew he was right but wasn't ready to hear the truth. All my life I'd wanted my parents to love me, and I couldn't face the fact that they didn't, that they'd all but forgotten me a long time ago.

On June 25, 1990, my friend Pat and her family came to my house for dinner. As we began to talk about the things that had happened in my past, I began to think about how it might have been for me if I'd had a different childhood and parents who loved me. Two months before that I'd learned from the police that it was Mr. And Mrs. Pat McCarthy who had been my foster parents. They had resided at Grand Falls but were now in the nearby town of Windsor. They gave me the phone number. So many times I wanted to take that step forward and call them. But I always changed my mind at the last minute. I was afraid that they wouldn't want anything to do with me. I asked my friend that day what she thought.

She said, "If I were them, I'd want to hear from you." Then she added, "What's the worst thing that can happen— they tell you they don't want to see you? Are you going to be any worse off than you are now?"

I said, "Maybe they won't remember me."

My friend looked at me skeptically. With a raised eyebrow, she merely said, "really?"

I shrugged and said, "Oh, I'll think about it for a while."

"Don't wait too long," She warned. "These people can't be young."

After my friend went home that evening, I made the call. A man answered the phone. It was Mr. McCarthy, Pat. I explained how I had gotten the number and then went on to ask if they were foster parents about twenty-five years ago. Mr. McCarthy said that they had been. I introduced myself as Sandra Brown and told him that his wife had taken care of me for a year. He told me his wife, Mary, had had a bad fall and was in a seniors' home. But he was eager to meet me.

He said, "So you're the little Brown girl from Norris arm?"

I said, "Yes, sir. You're right about that."

We set up a meeting for the following Wednesday.

On June 27, 1990, the day I went to Windsor to see Mr. McCarthy, I was very nervous. I didn't know how we'd react when we saw each other. Sitting in the car, I realized I had to go through with this. I couldn't turn back now. When I got to the door, the thought was still in my mind to turn back, but I gave a little knock anyway. A man came to the door and welcomed me into the house.

I said, "My name is Sandra." Entering, I looked curiously around the house, searching in vain for something familiar to link to my childhood. As we sat down to talk, I didn't know exactly what to say. I just looked at him, trying to recognize his face, but I couldn't remember seeing him before.

I asked him if this was the house that I had lived in. He said, "No, the one we had then was a big white one." He continued, "There was a fire." He went on to tell me of how they had lost a little boy in a wheelchair in the fire. "We had twenty-two children at that time," He explained. "two of them were newborn twin sisters. I was away working, and Mary was here alone with the children. She got all the rest of them out in time." He stopped to collect himself and then continued. "But it was too late to save the house. The fire moved fast through that old house. Mary couldn't reach the boy in time and the fire took his life."

I felt guilty in making him recall these painful events. But I was so thirsty for details of my childhood that I urged him to continue.

"after the fire," He went on, "we built this house."

I said, "I didn't think it was the same one. I can remember there was a store across from the house." Then I asked him about a white stove because I remembered that one day a teapot had broken there and the tea leaves had run down over the side. "I was so afraid and started to cry," I said. "But the lady picked me up and said, 'That's okay, Sandra. It's not your fault. The teapot just broke.'" I continued: "Then she sat in her rocking chair beside the white stove and held me in her arms and rocked me like I was her baby. I felt so secure and cared for. It was the first time I wasn't blamed for something bad happening."

Mr. McCarthy sighed. "Yes, that would be my Mary," He said. "She loved every one of those kids as if they were her own. It was one of the saddest moments of her life when children's aid told us we were too old to have foster kids anymore. I still hear from many of those kids. They call or stop by just to talk about their time with us. Mary always got Mother's Day cards from lots of them. In many ways she was more a mother to them than their biological mothers."

"I wish I could remember her face," I said. "as much as I feel the love in her heart, I can't remember what she looked like."

We continued to talk as Mr. McCarthy made me a coffee. As I drank, Mr. McCarthy told me that I had been removed from their care because my mother didn't like it that they belonged to the catholic church. One day a lady came and took me away from their home. The McCarthys had thought I'd been placed in another foster home. They didn't know I'd gone back to live with my parents until I told him.

I asked him about his wife. Mr. McCarthy told me that her legs had gotten weak and that she'd had a bad fall and broken her hip. He said sadly, "I don't think she'll be coming back home to live anymore. It broke my heart to have to put her in a home," He said, with tears in his eyes. "But it was the best thing to do. She's getting the care she needs. She's weak, and i'm too old to be able to care for her at home. But I go every day to see her. I keep hoping that one day she'll be strong enough and well enough to want to come home. Right now she's content to be where trained staff can look after her." He blew his nose and wiped his eyes.

I said, "If you don't mind, I'd like to come back and visit you again. I'd like for us to keep in touch. It took so long to find you, and I don't want to lose you again."

He looked at me and said, "The door to my home will always be open for you."

My eyes filled with tears as I listened to the words of love coming from his mouth. What a feeling, to finally meet one of my foster parents after twenty-six years of roaming around in the world wondering who they were, where they lived, and whether they would want anything to do with me. So many wasted years of not knowing!

It was a wonderful moment in my life. Visiting with Mr. McCarthy, I was able to find some of the missing pieces in my life and to uncover a dark secret that had never been told to me. Over the years I'd heard people talk about how I'd been removed from my parents' home for a time, but I'd never been told why or where I'd lived after I'd been taken away. I vowed I would keep in touch with the McCarthys.

On June 28, 1990, I went to Guy Memorial Hospital to meet Mrs. Mary McCarthy. On my way to the little town of Buchans, I kept wondering if she'd remember me. It had been so many years. What would she do when she saw me? What would I do? I felt so happy, like a little girl. We were going to meet again for the first time in twenty-six years.

My dream was coming true. I felt so excited. My mind was running wild.

At the hospital a male nurse said, "Mary is in the first room. She's in the bed beside the window."

I thanked him and started walking toward the room. A man approached and asked if I was Mary's grandchild.

I replied, "No, I'm one of Mary's foster children. I don't know if she'll remember me. It's been twenty-six years."

I told him my name. He walked to the foot of Mary's bed and said, "Mary, do you remember Sandra? Sandra Brown from your fostering days?"

The woman in the bed didn't say a word but just stared at him, not blinking. It seemed as if she hadn't heard him. I could hardly stand my disappointment. My friend's admonishment about waiting too long echoed in my mind. I was thinking that now there was no way she could know who I was.

But I had to give it one more shot before turning around and walking away. I looked at the man and said, "can I talk to her?" Then I approached her bed and said, "Mrs. McCarthy? It's Sandra Brown, the little girl from Norris Arm. Do you remember rocking me after the teapot broke?"

At the sound of my words she turned her head toward me, reached her hands out to me and said, "I didn't want to let you go. But they said your parents wanted you back. So I had to let you go. You were always in my mind, night and day. Thank God you're alive! I am so glad you found me."

With tears in my eyes, I said, "Yes, I'm glad I found you, too. I wish I'd found you years ago. I could have helped you out—done something for you."

She just looked at me and smiled. As her eyes looked into mine, I could see the joy and love in them. She held my hands tight and said, "It was God who brought you back to me. You were such a good baby. You never said anything, not one cross word."

I stood there at her bedside, trying hard not to cry. I was so happy! She told me about how, when she would take me for a walk down the road, she would tell people about me. "This is my little girl," She'd say. "I was so proud of you. I'm glad to have you back."

I left the hospital promising to visit her again soon. I could tell my two-hour visit had elated but tired her. She was so thin and frail.

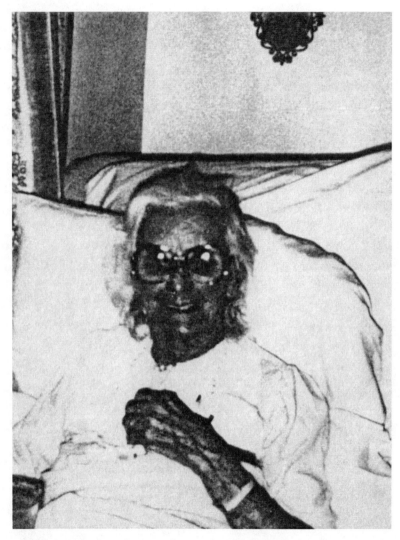

Meeting with Mrs. McCarthy

Despite the wonderful visit, I left the hospital that day feeling sad, thinking how nice it would have been if I had gotten to stay with the McCarthys. Instead Mother managed to get me back and abuse me all over again. It gave me one more reason to hate her.

All sorts of thoughts about my mother raged through my mind. I hated her. She had never been a real mother to me. She couldn't even look at me without hitting me with things like belts, sticks, skipping ropes, knives, and broom handles. There were even times when my parents used the same whip that Father used on the horse. Showing no mercy, they brought that whip down across my back, bringing blood each time.

So many times before, I'd sit and dream about ways to kill my own parents. Night after night I'd go to bed thinking of ways to pull it off. I thought about shooting them. But that, I decided, would be too fast. They wouldn't feel enough pain. I would imagine having them in the basement of my house, hanging there crying out for help. I imagined myself whipping them over and over again and watching the blood pour from their beaten bodies. I thought about stabbing them, making little cuts in their skin to make them suffer and feel how painful it is to have your skin cut. I would fantasize about seeing them go hungry as I sat in front of them eating and hearing them beg me to feed them. I'd drop crumbs on the floor and watch as they crawled on their knees to pick it up and put it in their mouths because they were so hungry. I wanted to kill them slowly and watch them die a little each day until they were both dead. I wanted them to feel the pain that I'd had to endure through-out my life. Over time I came to realize that these thoughts were just voices in my head that I needed to control. Of course, vengeful actions of this kind would not only be wrong in themselves but would do me and those I loved no good.

The darkness now overtakes my light. I try hard not to feel, As I toss and turn throughout the night.

My body is numb inside me, As I struggle to put my feet to the floor. I feel someone pushing me As I walk through my bedroom door.

I cry, "God, help me make it Across the cold, hard floor!"

And, once again, I fight. For that dark world must not Overtake my light.

Justice Prevails

CHAPTER SIXTEEN
FULL CIRCLE

When I returned to Newfoundland, I began working as a house-keeper. During that time the stress of trying to deal with my past brought on a nervous breakdown, and I was encouraged by one of my clients to visit a doctor. To this doctor I finally opened up about my hellish childhood. With the help of Dr. Neil Sheppard from Lewisporte, I eventually went to the police with my story. My parents were charged with child abuse that spanned two decades of physical, mental, and verbal abuse and neglect.

My brother and sisters supported my efforts at first but eventually turned their backs on me in favour of my parents. Once again I found myself alone. Somewhere inside me, though, I found a hidden courage to carry on.

My testimony led to a lengthy legal case that gained province-wide media attention. My mother was tried first, and her trial ended in august 1992. Mother was sentenced to two months' incarceration for child abuse and failing to provide the necessities of life. Judge Abe Schwartz said that the sentence was minimal because of Mother's medical condition. (She had high blood pressure.) The crown then appealed the judge's decision, and my mother was in the end sentenced to a total of eighteen months of incarceration.

In November 1992 I moved to New Brunswick to make yet another new start. Later I returned to Newfoundland for the trial of my father, only to find my siblings still standing by my parents like bodyguards. I stood off to the side all alone, as if I were a stranger to these people who had grown up watching our parents beat me, verbally abuse me, and lock me up in a tiny, dark room with no food or warmth.

I still have so many unanswered questions:

Why was I kept in that little box? Was it meant to be my last resting place? Why just me, out of a family of nine children? Why was I given back to my parents? Why did people not report what they saw? Where was that little Black room in the house? Why was I kept in that room, locked away from the family? Why wasn't I given food like the rest of the family?

Why didn't they feel my pain? Why were my parents not charged when I was taken away and placed in foster care?

Why did the justice system fail me when I was a child? The writing was on the wall, but they overlooked everything,

CHAPTER SEVENTEEN
FROM THE TRIAL TRANSCRIPTS

<u>Complainant:</u>
Sandra Brown (married name, Sandra Pelley), daughter
Accused:
Mrs. Breta Naomi Brown (biological mother)
Accused:
Mr. Theodore Brown (biological father)
Judge:
The Honourable Mr. Schwartz
Crown Attorney:
Mr. Matthews
Defence Attorney:
Mr. Black

<u>Witnesses:</u>
Dr. Neil Sheppard:
First person to make police report about the abuse
Dr. Anderson:
Plastic surgeon
Dr. Twomey:
Family doctor
Dr. Martin:

Worked with Dr. Twomey From the testimony of Dr. Ross L. Martin

Mr. Matthews. Dr. Martin, you are a practising physician, are you?
Dr. Martin. Yes sir. [...]
Mr. Matthews.
And how long have you been practising here in Grand Falls-Windsor?
Dr. Martin. It will be twenty-nine years come February 1993.
Mr. Matthews.
And in connection with matters before the court, where were you [at the time of the events in question]?
Dr. Martin.
[...] I was assistant Medical Health Officer at Botwood Cottage Hospital. [...]
Mr. Matthews.
Now, Doctor, with respect to a patient, Sandra Mae Brown, at that time, I understand you had occasion to be the attending physician for that child.
Dr. Martin. That's right. [...]
Mr. Matthews.
What was your involvement with Sandra Mae Brown at that point in time?
Dr. Martin.
Well, in that particular admission to hospital, I was the attending physician during her stay. [...] She was initially admitted on the 5th of June, 1963, to Dr. Twomey, and he did an initial assessment and then turned her care over to me. We [shared] responsibilities in those days at the hospital, and I treated most of the difficult paediatric problems, particularly those who needed intravenous feedings, that sort of thing. So he assessed her and then turned her over to me pretty promptly, and I took care of her after that time.
Mr. Matthews. What was that admission for?
Dr. Martin.

That admission was for, if we use the diagnosis on the chart ... The acute episode at that time, the final diagnosis, was hexia malnutrition. This was the diagnosis that was given at the time of discharge. At the time of admission the child was critically ill, near death, terribly emaciated [with] severe dehydration, which is a loss of body fluids.

Mr. Matthews.

Can you comment on her condition at that time? [...]

Dr. Martin.

I have the notes, but I still remember the child quite vividly after all these years. She was grossly underweight and malnourished for a child of her age. She was over four years of age at that time. [...] I remember the time well because we had so many cases at the time, and this child was admitted with a history of having two or three days of vomiting and profuse diarrhoea. [...] and the child at this particular admission too was extremely ill, severely dehydrated. She was listless and lethargic, with sunken eyes and gross weight loss, exhibited evidence of dehydration. [...] and I notice from my notes that at that time there were some bruises over her face and forehead and chin which could not be attributed to gastroenteritis. [...]

Normally a child with dehydration you start [on] an intravenous. [With] a child that age you would put it in through a vein in the arm or the leg, or even the head if necessary. But this child obviously was quite ill to the point that I did a cut-down on the child. This is a procedure whereby you make an incision, usually in the leg, to isolate a vein, and you insert a tube, an intravenous tube, and place it because there is anticipation that the intravenous fluid requirement may be of a prolonged duration, and it becomes difficult to move the needle from site to site, so you put in more or less one that lasts longer. [...] So the child obviously was quite ill. And she made a fairly good recovery and was only in hospital ... I think she was only in about a week. Yes, and went home. [...]

Mr. Matthews.

What concerns [about bruising] did you have at that time, from your recollection?

Dr. Martin.

Well, I had some but they weren't ... as I remember, they weren't startling. I wondered about the bruising, but the child was not a child that I knew. I had not previously had any dealings with the child, and I remember discussing it with Dr. Twomey, who was my superior, wondering about it, because I think he more or less knew the family and knew the parents and dealt with them, but i'm [testifying] purely by recollection now. [...]

Mr. Matthews.

Perhaps you could go back and refresh the court with respect to [...] the admission of June 5, 1963.

Dr. Martin.

Yes, now this is [...] the admission that stays in my mind after all these years.

Mr. Matthews. Okay. What do you recollect, Doctor?

Dr. Martin.

I recollect that the child was in a terrible state of malnutrition and neglect, underweight, terribly ill, semicomatose, on the verge of death. In actual fact she weighed, as I find from the record, sixteen pounds, ten ounces, for a child that was four years and four months old.

Mr. Matthews. What would be the normal, would we expect?

Dr. Martin.

Well, you'd expect to be a lot more than that. I'm not even sure what the child's birth weight was, but I would have expected that child to weigh [...] probably thirty-five to forty pounds. A child of four years of age, depending on the birth weight and stature and size of the child. But certainly a lot more than the child was at the time that I saw it. And I can give a description from head to toe if you like.

Mr. Matthews. Yes, if you would, please.

Dr. Martin.

I remember it. Because these notes, the description here and the charts, your exhibit, is by Dr. Twomey [...] who did the initial assessment. But I did the hands-on treating of the child.

Mr. Matthews. Yes, if you can go through that, please.

Dr. Martin.

And she was, as I say, semi-comatose, near death, sunken eyes, thin, straggly, listless, lustreless hair, which was sparse. She had lice, her head was caked with dirt, scabs and sores, and she had—this is again a recollection—she had a little indentation on her lip which I still remember. I've seen her since here in the courtroom. It's not as obvious to look at her now as it appeared to me looking at her then. [as] a little child she seemed to have a little dimple on one side of her lip, and I didn't know exactly what it was, if it was a birth defect or a laceration which had been inflicted and didn't heal properly because of no medical treatment.

Mr. Matthews. Did you recall that from 1961, having seen it then?

Dr. Martin.

No, I don't recall [...] having seen it then, and I think had it been there, I would have commented on it in my notes.

Mr. Matthews. [...] You were describing her basically head to toe.

Dr. Martin.

Yes. She had bruising, facial bruising. Her ribs were protruding. You could count her ribs at a distance. It was just skin over bone. Her abdomen was sunken, scaphoid, so thin the abdominal peristaltic movements of the bowel [were visible] through her skin. [as for] her extremities [...] the most prominent parts were the joints, practically no muscle mass whatsoever. The skin that was thin, stretched over this skeleton practically, bruising on the extremities, dirt on the extremities and a general state of chronic I would say malnutrition, and in addition to this an acute overbearing severe dehydration, which was the life-threatening thing at that moment.

Mr. Matthews.

You mentioned malnutrition. [...] What period of time are you looking at [...]?

Dr. Martin. Well, looking at [it], I have to assume the child had Reasonable health other than the acute episodes to hospital. [...] The admissions to hospital were, one, for gastroenteritis. [Then] a subsequent one to Dr. Twomey for abdominal distention. I don't know anything about that one. And this one, there's a child of four years of age, weighing sixteen pounds and a few ounces, with no muscle mass [...], [it] was very obvious that this was a chronic state of malnutrition, and on top of that was superimposed an acute dehydration, or maybe it was a dehydration which had developed over several days, but it had reached a point that it was life-threatening, that she would have died without appropriate treatment within probably hours, a couple of hours. [...] She was near death.

Mr. Matthews.

You mentioned lack of muscle. Would that be short-term?

Dr. Martin.

No, that would be long-term. This [...] is the indicator that this was of long standing.

Mr. Matthews. Okay, the dehydration could be of shorter [standing]?

Dr. Martin.

I mean, if she had good muscle mass and dehydration that's a different ... but this was a situation of obvious long-standing lack of nutrition, to produce the state of wasting which was generalized from head to toe.

Mr. Matthews. You also indicated bruising?

Dr. Martin.

There was bruising, bluish marks [on the] extremities. I'm not sure about buttocks, but I know extremities. I know [on the] face. I recall that, and probably other areas as well. Mr. Matthews. What would you attribute that to? Dr. Martin. I attribute it to neglect in view of the fact that the state of the child was in a state of dirt, neglect, and lice and sores. I mean, a child [with] that going on, a chronic state like that, I would have thought would have long ago been treated by a physician had she been looked [after] properly. [...]

Mr. Matthews. How did she respond to nutrition?

Dr. Martin.

At the beginning she was rather slow. The initial treatment involved intravenous fluids and vitamins and antibiotics to get her over the life-threatening dehydration. Once this was corrected, it was a matter of getting her on a nutritional program to give her body requirements and to get her to feed like a normal child. At first she would only take bread, water, tea. She didn't seem to like anything else. She would refuse other things. She wouldn't take milk at first. She wouldn't take juices. She wouldn't take other things.

Mr. Matthews. Can you comment on that at all?

Dr. Martin.

Well, my own feeling was that [...] probably she'd never really had them before. I felt her diet probably had consisted of bread and tea or water because she liked these. She asked for these things. And given new things, she didn't like them. But with persuasion and kindness from the staff, she eventually started eating ravenously and she ate almost anything offered.

Now some of the nursing staff could probably comment on that better than I, but I remember these things because she received a tremendous amount of care and love from our whole staff. [...] She became the pet of the hospital and everybody sort of had a great feeling of kindness and love towards her, and she really thrived on it.

Mr. Matthews.

Can you comment on her reaction to people in the initial stages?

Dr. Martin.

She seemed to be frightened and scared and intimidated very easily, but after a few days she readily accepted love and attention, and you know, she was a little pet around the hospital ward, and it's amazing the change in the child in a short time and how quickly she gained weight. In a period of four to five weeks she gained approximately ten pounds.

Mr. Matthews. Other foods were introduced into her diet?

Dr. Martin.

Yes. I don't recall what. [...] I'm aware of the early stages because there were difficulties in feeding the child, but [...] she certainly responded and ate well, obviously. At discharge she was somewhere around twenty-four or twenty-six pounds, and that was five weeks later. The discharge date was the 12th of July, 1963. So she was in hospital approximately five weeks.

Mr. Matthews.

You've indicated that on the 6th there was a crying for bread.

Dr. Martin.

Yes. One ounce of milk was offered, but the child only drank half an ounce. Said she didn't like it. That was a nursing note.

Mr. Matthews. But your recollection ...

Dr. Martin.

My recollection is that she thrived. Her little face filled out. She had more lustre to her hair. She [became] a short, chubby little girl. She was beginning to fill out and looked like a normal little human being, and I can see her ... they used to carry her around with them on the wards, and they'd sit her up on the scales. There were lots of pictures taken of her by various members of the staff down there. And she was a different child just within a few days.

Mr. Matthews.

Here we have a comment—it's just an example—on the 19th of June. Scab removed from back of head?

Dr. Martin.

This is one of the scabs on her head. There is a granulation treated with silver nitrate. That meant it was almost a sore with raw, probably bleeding tissue when the scab came off, so the treatment then was to burn this with a chemical to stop the bleeding and produce granulation. In other words it was a sore, but I'm not sure where it was. It was on the back of her head, but she had many of these caked sores on her.

Mr. Matthews.

Did you have any further dealings with Sandra Mae Brown?

Dr. Martin. No.

Mr. Matthews.

Those are all the questions I have of the doctor. My friend may have some.

The Court. Thank you, Mr. Matthews. Mr. Black?

*

Mr. Black.

Thank you, my lord. Now with respect you've described the child's condition on June 5th when you first came into contact with her, and based on your experience how long would it take a child to reach that condition that you found her in when you first examined her? In other words was that a condition that occurred almost overnight, or would it take a significant amount of time?

Dr. Martin.

That's very difficult to answer, but the fact that there was so much wasting ... it could be a low degree of malnutrition over a fairly lengthy period of time, or it could be a more severe degree over a shorter period of time. But in any event it was over months. I'm quite sure it didn't happen overnight. Months maybe, or even longer. It could be low-grade chronic malnutrition over a year or more. It could have been a more severe degree of malnutrition over a shorter period of time. But nevertheless it would have been of rather long standing I think. Not overnight. Not in a week or two. It would be many weeks or months, I would think.

Mr. Black.

And say, generally speaking, as a normal healthy person with no symptoms of malnutrition, based on experience, would you be able to say how long it would take a person of normal average health to deteriorate to the stage of the condition that you found this child to be in?

Dr. Martin. I think it would take a long period of time. I'm basing this on the fact that the child had only minimal muscle tissue and skin. There was no ... like, we have subcutaneous tissue of fat and things underneath. That was all gone. In other words, any that the child might have been able to accumulate was lost. And the muscles were lost. That means either she never did have any or she had them and they were slowly metabolized to keep her going.

So I think the period of time was lengthy. We found no evidence of any other disease in this child. She had acute dehydration which was treated in a matter of a day with intravenous feedings. She was put on proper oral nutrition.

Mr. Black.

So basically I take it from your evidence, Dr. Martin, that the tell-tale sign or symptom so to speak would be the wasting of the skin?

Dr. Martin.

The general wasting of the skin, you see [in] a child even in these days from poor backgrounds, [but] we never saw children in that state, caked with sores and bruises and lice and wasting and mal-nutrition. I mean we saw children with vitamin deficiencies who were plump, fat little children but because the parents didn't know how to feed them properly, they didn't get vitamin c and that, scurvy. But they were not neglected children. This was more than coincidence to my estimation.

Mr. Black.

I know it's a difficult question to answer, but for my own purposes I've been trying to determine the time frame that may be involved.

Dr. Martin. I'm sorry I can't give you precise time, but it's lengthy.

Mr. Black.

It would be over months, probably, this degree of wasting?

Dr. Martin. It would not occur, as I say, in a matter of a few days.

Mr. Black.

So basically would it be fair to say that if you accept the fact that it may take a matter of months, essentially if it did in fact take a matter of months, then the food intake would be almost negligible?

Dr. Martin. It would have to be below nutritional requirements.

Mr. Black.

When you say nutritional requirements, what exactly do you mean?

Dr. Martin.

Well, a person, we all have a certain nutritional requirement that meets your daily needs and enables us to [inaudible] ... an adequate amount which balances what we expend each day, our weight stays stable. If we eat excessively, we gain weight, and if we eat insufficiently, we lose weight.

But you don't waste away overnight. You don't lose your muscle mass overnight.

Mr. Black.

Thank you, Doctor, that's what I thought. But Sandra Pelley was in fact gone beyond that stage.

Dr. Martin. Yes.

Mr. Black.

And on the admission in June of 1963 do you recall who it was that admitted the child?

Dr. Martin. No.

Mr. Black. Do the records indicate who it was?

Dr. Martin.

No. There was some unusual circumstances surrounding her admission, as I'm going by recollection now. There's no documentation that I have available to me, but the story ... there's something in my mind that tells me that somewhere I have the impression that this child was found in this state in the home in a carnation milk carton box, somewhere near the stove in this neglected state.

Mr. Black. But your main concerns for your opinion that it went on for a significant period of time and not a short term was the tell-tale symptom of poor skin mass, skin ...

Dr. Martin.

Yes, general condition of the child indicated a chronic state of malnutrition.

Mr. Black. Muscle mass.

Dr. Martin.

Yes, muscle mass, skin turgor, texture of hair. There were many, you know, other features, but this was a long [...] ongoing thing, I think. With life-threatening dehydration on top of it.

Mr. Black.

So I suppose in the end in the process, you just have the vital organs and [are] near death?

Dr. Martin.

Yes. You are left with vital organs and you have some muscle mass and skin. This child just had thin skin over wasted muscles. No subcutaneous tissue whatsoever.

Mr. Black.

So in your time as a physician have you ever seen anything like this?

Dr. Martin.

No, never before or since. Never. That's why it's so ... it still lingers with me. I don't think she would have withstood a very lengthy period of dehydration, certainly to the degree that was present here. [She] was critical, on the verge of death. A dying child.

*

Sentencing Decision of Mr. Justice Schwartz

The accused, Breta Naomi Brown, has been found guilty of the offence of common assault contrary to section 231(1) (a) of the criminal code of canada as it then was and the further offence of failing to provide the necessaries of life to a child under the age of sixteen years contrary to Section 186(2) (a) (i) of the code as it was then numbered. At the time of these offences both carried with them liability to imprisonment of up to two years. The offence now of 231(1) (a) with its amendments I believe carries with it the liability today up to a longer period, up to five years.

The victim in each of the matters was the accused's daughter presently named Sandra Pelley. Ms. Pelley is presently thirty-three years of age. The offences occurred in the 1960's when the victim was a young child between eight and eleven years old.

The facts indicate that during this period the complainant was constantly beaten by the accused, frequently separated from family members, isolated by being placed in a room by herself and given little to eat. There were occasions when the complainant was not permitted to eat during mealtime. This is some of the evidence that was heard by this court and I find [...] very little merit in again repeating the graphic descriptions which were brought forth in the testimony of the complainant.

The offender, Naomi Brown, is presently fifty-one years of age. She was married in 1956 at the age of sixteen years. That marriage produced eleven children of which two died in birth in the 1960's. Since the laying of these charges the accused has separated from her husband and she has been living a common law relationship for the past two years.

I am satisfied on the evidence and the Pre-sentence report that the whole tenure of the accused's marriage has been one of financial difficulty because of a large family living on what I would term minimal income. The accused's children did not have any of the luxuries of life or any of the other material items which were experienced oftentimes by other children. Nevertheless, that does not excuse Mrs. Brown from the cruel manner in which she raised the complainant treating her in a word I would describe as an "outcast" From the other family members.

In any family unit although material items may be lacking because of financial difficulty, and that's somewhat common at times, a parent is still able to bestow the greater gifts of love, affection, guidance and protection to a child. Although there is nothing in the evidence to suggest the accused did not give this to her other children these attributes were certainly lacking in her attitude toward the complainant at what I would term the most crucial time in the complainant's life, her childhood. There has been a denial to the victim Mrs. Pelley by her mother and undoubtedly she will always bear the scars of this betrayal for the rest of her life.

Criminal actions against children are probably the most reprehensible and repugnant matters which come before a court. A young victim is completely vulnerable and unprotected. That vulnerability is further penetrated when the aggressor is a parent, a person in whom the victim should be able to trust and seek protection. When this is lacking from a parent then it's obvious the other joys of childhood are forever destroyed.

In this matter i've heard submissions from counsel and the crown seeks a period of incarceration of seventeen months to two years on the facts that were presented. The accused argues that the offences occurred some twenty to thirty years ago and this court should give consideration to this fact together with Mrs. Brown's circumstances at the time and argues that a probationary period or a brief period of incarceration would not be an inappropriate sentence.

I have considered the submissions of counsel. As well I have read all of the cases that were cited and I think counsel can agree with me the cases, although they present some light as to how courts come about in sentencing, a lot of the cases referred to, most of them in fact, had reference to sexual assaults or situations where there was abuse to the point of criminal negligence and I believe in one case cited even to the degree of manslaughter.

A sentencing court must never lose sight of the charge which is before the court and in this case I am faced with one charge of common assault and I am faced with one charge of failing to provide the necessaries of life.

As well I think I can say that the charge of failing to provide the necessaries of life although brought under the criminal code the court can surmise, although the court does not go beyond the reason for why it would have been brought under the code as opposed to other remedies which would have been appropriate under the Welfare of children act, nevertheless these are the two charges before me and these are the charges upon which I must sentence the accused.

In this matter I found the following to be what I term aggravating factors.

1. The accused's attitude toward this whole affair. I am satisfied that it's totally lacking in remorse. That was determined by both the evidence and followed by the Presentence report. The accused, Mrs. Brown, does not accept what she has done to her child. For whatever reason there just doesn't seem to be acceptance.

2. The second thing which I find to be aggravating is the fact that Mrs. Brown, the accused, was not only the aggressor but she was the natural parent of the victim. She was the person holding the highest form of trust which society can bestow on an individual.

These I find to be very aggravating factors.

In addition to those factors I have also had to consider the following which I would term mitigating factors. One of those [which] the court has placed a great emphasis on in determining an appropriate sentence is the fact that the offence is now twenty-five to thirty years old. That has to be given some consideration with some other matters.

As well the complainant is now an adult. Her testimony is that she has at times since reaching adulthood [...] formed some relationship with her mother. Whether that relationship exists today or not this court is uncertain.

But since the episodes and since she has become an adult she has formed some relationship with her mother and the accused has attended to the complainant's children at the complainant's request.

I have also given some consideration to the health of Mrs. Brown. There is indication that she has an arthritic condition, high blood pressure, bone deterioration and possibly some psychiatric problems.

In cases involving any form of abuse toward a child I am satisfied that the primary principles to be considered by a sentencing court are that of public protection and deterrence, both general and specific. Obviously in this case the protection of the complainant and specific deterrence are no longer required. Nevertheless, consideration must be given to general public protection and general deterrence such that crimes against children such as this can be eradicated in today's society and they are principles which I have considered in deeming the appropriate sentence for Mrs. Brown.

General public deterrence and general public protection and deterrence are best achieved in my opinion through some period of incarceration. In circumstances of this case as I have stated considerable consideration has been given to the fact that the offences are twenty-five to thirty years old. If these offences were to come before this court going back in the past year or two the offences would be inexcusable and the sentence I can assure any member of the public and particularly the accused would be considerably higher than that which I have determined to be appropriate for this before me.

Again Mrs Brown is there anything you wish to say?

I have also considered that the accused and the victim have gone on with their lives, although I am satisfied Ms. Pelley has gone on bearing emotional scars. I am further satisfied Mrs. Brown is not now a threat to anyone.

Giving consideration to everything I am sentencing the accused to two Months imprisonment on each offence. Sentences are to run concurrently. I am placing her on probation for a period of One Year with the statutory conditions, that she keep the peace and be of good behaviour. She is to report to a Probation Officer within seven days of release from Her Majesty's Penitentiary and thereafter as required. And she is to follow any form of counselling which might be recommended by the probation officer.

Pursuant to Sections 737(4), 738(4) and 740(4) of the criminal code I would advise you Mrs. Brown that while bound by this Probation Order if you should be convicted of another offence including one of failure to comply with this Order in addition to any other punishment that may be imposed the conditions of this Order may be varied.

I am directing that the Probation Order be read over to the accused and she be provided with a copy of same.

I have also given some consideration to whether I was going to impose a victim Surcharge Fine but in view of the sentence and the financial circumstances of the accused I see little merit in it and I am not going to impose it.

Is there anything else counsel wish to raise?

Mr. Matthews. Nothing, my lord.

*

Mother's case was appealed, and she was subsequently sentenced to eighteen months.

*

Decision of Lewis, J., Regarding Theodore Brown

Now I want to thank you both for your submissions. To turn to the matter of the consideration of the evidence and the charges that are before the court I will do what counsel has done and start with the second count on the indictment which I will read.

And it says that between the 1st day of January, a.d. 1962 and the 1st day of January, a.d. 1968 at or near Peterview in the Province of Newfoundland being the parent of Sandra Brown, a child under the age of sixteen years, did fail without lawful excuse to provide the necessaries of life to Sandra Brown then being in necessitous circumstances contrary to section 186.2 (a) (i) of the criminal code of canada.

Now we must turn to Section 186. It says everyone is under a legal duty as a parent, foster parent, guardian or head of a family to provide necessaries of life for a child under the age of sixteen years. And it goes on to deal with other Sections which don't apply here. But that is the gist and the heart of the case. That if you are a parent or a foster parent, parent in this case, you have a legal duty, a duty imposed by law to provide the necessaries of life to a child.

Now we then ask the question what are the necessaries of life? Well the necessaries of life are obviously food and water. They can be medical care. They can be a variety of things depending on what a child needs in order to, not just to survive but to live and be brought up in a proper manner according to the customs and the ways of our society. But certainly food is a basic necessity and in our society medical care which is available in this country that also we consider to be a necessity and one of the necessaries of life.

[...] Sandra was born in 1959 and when she was approximately four years old and a bit she was admitted to hospital and Dr. Martin was a physician in the hospital in Botwood at the time. The actual admission of Sandra Brown was handled by Dr. Twomey who is now deceased and he made notes at the time and we have the benefit of these notes. But the most important evidence is the evidence of Dr. Martin who was there in the hospital and it was he to whom Dr. Twomey passed over the matter of the care of Sandra Brown. And Dr. Martin thirty years later has sworn in his evidence that in all of his thirty years what he was asked by Dr. Twomey to deal with, namely the case of Sandra Brown, was the worse and most serious case that he had come across in his whole thirty years of the practice of medicine, so serious that he can see it now in his mind's eye with the same clarity that he could see it then.

Now what was it that Dr. Twomey passed over to Dr. Martin to look after? What case? It was Sandra Brown, child, but it was a case and we cannot mince words here, it was a case of a child starved to within hours of the point of death. Now that's what it was. And the evidence is absolutely clear on that and there is no way to mince words or call it anything other than what it was. Someone had starved that child to the point almost of death because Dr. Martin said in his evidence, he said the child would have died soon without the medical care that we gave her. It could have been he said a matter of two hours or a few more hours. She was dehydrated but in addition to that she had been starved because her bones were sticking out through her joints, her skin was thin, you could see the workings of the organs inside her body through her skin. That's what he said. And of course it's not surprising finding what he found that he remembers it with this clarity which he does thirty years later. The child at the time was sixteen pounds ten ounces. A child of that age would normally be expected to be between thirty and forty pounds. It wasn't a short term thing such as may occur with dehydration when a child or an adult for that matter but especially a child gets suddenly ill becomes dehydrated and loses some pounds of weight.

That wasn't the case at all. It was a case of systematic and continuing deprivation of food that had brought the child to that state. And from the evidence which Dr. Martin gave there is absolutely no doubt at all as to what brought the child to the state. In addition the child was in a filthy state, covered with scabs and sores, and it was obviously to the doctor, and I find that it in fact was so on the basis of his evidence, that the child had been starved and completely neglected as well. The hospital kept her for some weeks, five or six weeks. They brought her back to health by feeding her. She wasn't used to eating most of the foods that they provided. The only food that she was used to apparently or seemed to be used to was bread. But by feeding her, caring for her, they brought her back to health, to a decent weight, so that at the end of the five or six week period they had a normal quite healthy child, and she was saved obviously from death by the efforts of the people in the hospital at Botwood.

Now the matter was then brought to the attention of the Provincial court in Grand Falls and the then Magistrate cramm made an order declaring Sandra a neglected child and she was placed in foster care and she stayed there for some months. So it was almost a year later when she was brought back to her home.

So we must then examine what happened there. Now Sandra Brown, Sandra Pelley as she is now, gave evidence and she said her memories of childhood and she doesn't remember anything before she went to hospital but she remembers afterwards. She remembers living life in a dark room where she was kept as a prisoner except when she started school, she was allowed out to go to school, but she was kept as a prisoner in a dark room and fed bread when she was fed at all. So not only had someone denied her the necessities of life, namely food and medical care before she went into hospital, but she was systematically denied the necessities of life after she came back from foster care and into the home at Norris Arm, her parents' home. She was systematically denied proper food and medical care right throughout the period that is referred to in the indictment. Her evidence is quite clear and I will say quite clearly that I believe her evidence because her evidence has been corroborated by a great deal of evidence from other sources, some of it reluctant and some of it only partially, but her evidence has none the less been corroborated but I found her as a witness to be frank and clear and she told of accounts which I am satisfied were correct. So that throughout the years after she was brought home she was systematically denied proper food because this family was not a destitute family, this family had food, she was denied that food. And she was also denied medical care.

Now this goes to the matter of the assaults which I will deal with later but I think we have to be very clear that serious assaults were committed, and I will deal with that later, on Sandra Brown but also becomes very clear from the evidence that she didn't get the medical care. She was again denied the necessities of life and I will for the moment allude to one incident only. She was beaten by her mother severely with a belt and her mother used the buckle as the end to administer the beating. The beating injured her eye and she was two years without medical treatment while her eye ran with water and latterly with inflammation or pus as she described it, without medical care and at the end of that period she was blind in that eye. Now it should have been obvious to anyone there and in any position of authority that this child had something seriously wrong with her eye and yet she was denied medical care until another family member eventually intervened and she got that care. So she was denied food and care before she went into hospital. On her return she was also over a period of years denied food, proper food, that is proper nourishment and proper care and medical attention.

Now the evidence is absolutely clear that this took place. There is the evidence of the doctor. There is the evidence of Sandra Pelley herself and there is enough evidence from the other family members who gave evidence and from the accused himself to confirm that this was basically the case so that I am satisfied completely without any question of doubt that she was so deprived of the necessaries of life.

So then we turn to the question who deprived her? Who had the responsibility for making sure that that child had the necessities of life? Well she had two parents and both of these parents were there living with her and she under their care in their house in Norris Arm and subsequently in Peterview. So that the people who had the responsibility were unquestionably Mr. Brown, the accused here, and his wife Mrs. Brown.

Now the section says everyone is under a legal duty as a parent to provide necessaries of life for a child under the age of sixteen years. She had a duty, Mrs. Brown. He had a duty, Mr. Brown. Now he described what happened and Sandra described and the other children who gave evidence describe what happened and it's quite obvious that Mrs. Brown whose mentality I cannot fathom and no explanation has been given to me nor will I venture to suggest explanations but for some reason Mrs. Brown had a terrible dislike or hatred for Sandra. She apparently was the prime mover the prime source of the starvation and the beatings with which I'll deal later. But it's interesting the explanation that has been given in part by the other children who gave evidence and the explanation that Mrs. Brown hated Sandra perhaps because she stood up for herself. But that explanation doesn't explain why Sandra was starved almost to the point of death as a three or four year old. It might explain something not justified but it might explain it when a person was older but why did Mrs. Brown choose to be the prime mover in starving Sandra to death almost to death when she was three/four years old?

Now what was Mr. Brown's role in this, the accused? Well Mr. Brown was there. He was the father of the child. There was no doubt about that. He knew it, knew perfectly well that this was his child, in his family, in his home and he allowed the child to sink almost to the point of death and did nothing. It is true that he was frightened of his wife. I am prepared to believe that, but that's not a sufficient excuse for what transpired. It's not a sufficient excuse to say well I wasn't home every day all day long. That's not a sufficient excuse. He was home on a frequent basis. He was home sometimes. When there was no work he was home throughout and other times he was only home on weekends but he was there and on many times many occasions he worked during the day in the woods and came home at night to the family home. So he was there. He had a duty to provide not only for that child

Sandra but also for his other children. But Sandra was not being provided for, whatever the case with the other children, i'm not dealing with that but Sandra was not provided for and he could not have lived in the same house without being aware that the child was not being provided for, that the child was being starved to death, and therefore he by doing nothing about it acquiesced in it because he was a parent just as much as Mrs. Brown was a parent and he had a duty provided by law to make sure that that child was properly fed and that that child did receive medical care, and when she was brought back again by the social worker almost a year later he had duty to ensure that she was properly fed, which she wasn't, and properly cared for in the sense of getting medical attention, which she did not get. That duty was there and it was a continuing duty that cannot be ignored and cannot be excused or sloughed off by saying someone else was in charge there and doing what was being done.

As a parent he too was in charge. So I am satisfied completely. It's not a question of weighing and balancing reasonable doubt. I am satisfied beyond a doubt Mr. Brown that you are guilty of failing to provide the necessaries of the necessities of life to Sandra Brown your daughter during the period mentioned in the indictment.

Now I move to the question of assault.

Now assault has been referred to. The charge is that on or about the 1st day of January, 1962 and the 1st day of January, 1972, that's a ten year span, at or near Peterview in the Province of Newfoundland did unlawfully commit a common assault on Sandra Brown contrary to Section 231.1(a) of the criminal code of canada.

Well 231.1(a) says everyone who commits a common assault is guilty of in this case of an indictable offence. And common assault is defined by the code and it said a person commits an assault when without the consent of another person or with that consent where it is obtained by fraud he applies force intentionally to the person of the other directly or indirectly.

Now what is the evidence? The evidence of Sandra Pelley which in its essence I accept as being true because it's corroborated also by other evidence before the court. The evidence is to put it simply and shortly that she was beaten to a pulp day after day, week after week, year after year. That is the evidence and everyone who has given evidence has corroborated that fact and said the same thing. She was beaten and beaten and beaten. Now there's no way to mince words about this. Counsel has very properly said well Section 43 of the criminal code, Section 43 gives parents the right to discipline children. But to apple the word discipline or correction to what went on in that house to my mind is a perversion of the language.

Discipline means that a parent when a child has done something wrong disciplines the child in a proper humane way to try and get the child to understand that what the child has done was not the right thing to do. The discipline can be physical as long as it's reasonable. It can take other forms which usually today probably are the usual ways of disciplining. But the point is that what went on according to the evidence in this household was not discipline as it's understood in Section 43 or as it's understood in our society.

This was savage beating unending, day after day, week after week. It wasn't discipline and Section 43 can't be used to suggest that this was some sort of proper discipline administered to a child to correct the child because of course the evidence is, not just of Sandra but of the other children who gave evidence, there didn't have to be a reason for the beatings for any of them. There didn't have to be a reason. The beatings were administered on a constant basis. Now we come back to Sandra Pelley's evidence. She says she was kept in the dark room, she was taken out, she was beaten and put back in there and it didn't have to be for any reason and this is corroborated by the others. It didn't have to be for a reason.

Now what about these beatings? Well these beatings weren't a slap on the bottom as a child often gets from a parent. These were beatings with weapons because what is a stick or horse leather if it's not a weapon? They were beatings administered by holding the child down and Mr. Brown does not admit this but I am satisfied that it's true that he would hold her with her head between his legs and holding her arms while two other children held her feet while Mrs. Brown beat her with a weapon, with a stick or a horse leather or whatever else that came to hand. Now this is what happened and I am satisfied beyond a reasonable doubt that it happened and i'm also satisfied that it could not be called discipline in any normal sense of the word that is contemplated by the criminal code of canada.

Now this went on and on and i'm just going to refer to the evidence which is before the court and this evidence is the Dr. Anderson who is a plastic surgeon who many years later in 1990 wrote this report and the report is in evidence. On examination, he's talking about, well to begin in the beginning of it: "This thirty-one year old woman was seen at the request of the R.C.M.P. She is apparently a victim of child abuse and I was asked to see her to determine whether it would be possible from assessing the scars to say whether they were caused by abuse." And he described her:

She is a short woman with a flat face on the left side and a glass eye. She has a whistle notch deformity of the lip reminiscent of cleft lip but on closer inspection shows there is no evidence of clefting. She has two scalp lacerations, one in the area of the lambdoid suture in the vertical area the other in the patch of bald skin approximately three centimetres in diameter in the left temporal parietal area which is the result of healing by secondary intentia. She has also a large defect in the soft tissues of the left hip measuring approximately 8–10 centimetres in length. This is deeply depressed by approximately 2–3 centimetres and is obviously the result of a soft tissue injury associated with bruising and fracturing of the fat with subsequent resorption and contracture of the skin. She has two faint lineal lacerations on the lateral aspect of the right and left thighs at the junction of the upper two-thirds and lower third of the thigh on either side. These are straight even lacerations which look like healed scalpel incisions or incisions made with a sharp instrument. It is much fainter on the left than on the right. These are well healed and flat wounds which would be the result of laceration or cut rather than bruising. The excellent healing and straightness of the laceration on the right especially which extends half way around the leg is not typical of laceration by glass for example or an accidental injury. She tells me she has no scars elsewhere.

The left eye was enucleated at age of eleven [...]. My first impression at looking at her was that she perhaps had a fracture of the maxilla on the left side of the fracture of the zygoma associated with an ocular injury which subsequently resulted in enucleation. Examination of the lip shows that there is a normal nose with a normal nostril cill bilaterally and normally formed communella with a normal filitrum. This negates the possibility of a cleft lip. Just lateral to the left edge of the columella there is a diagional scar about 1.5 centimetres in length. This is a well healed straight laceration. The central lip is very short. The vermilion border is intact but on everting the lip one sees that the fraenulum is destroyed.

There are multiple scars posteriorly and there is a retraction of the orbicularis oris muscle fibres in the area of the original wound so that the orbicularis is almost completely divided and joined only by thin scar tissue in the centre. There are small healed lacerations and tags of mucosa in the upper buccal celkis. Injury is not the result of the through and through laceration of the lip splitting the lip up to the root of the nose as is occasionally seen. There was undoubtedly some pentration of the outer skin as noted by the small diagonal laceration but the healed wound suggests bursting laceration such as a severe blow with rupture of the soft tissues against the underlying bony structures and teeth. The whole of the lip has been disrupted throughout its length from the lip to the nose and undoubtedly was held together only by the remaining intact skin from the outside. This injury has not received medical attention as there is no evidence of suture marks and no repair of the dehist orpercularis oris has been carried out.

The patient presents with an amazing variety of scars on various aspects of her body some of which at least do not appear to have received any medical attention. It is interesting that the patient confirms that she was admitted to hospital at the age of eleven. There is a medical record noting an injury to the lip but she is not aware of receiving any medical attention for this problem. The reason for the shortness of the lip in its verticle dimensions is associated with scar contracture and failure of growth in this area.

Now if there was any corroboration needed of what she herself has described and what the other children have described as for the beating, if there is any corroboration required it is provided by that report because what that report indicates is a series of injuries done to that woman over a period and that these injuries did not receive medical attention.

That's what that report says and the injuries were serious injuries, cutting, bruising, tearing of the tissue and we know about the injury to the eye which resulted in her losing her sight. So there is no question about the injuries. So we turn again to the question well who did these injuries? Certainly Mrs. Brown did the injuries. She was the prime mover but Mr. Brown you also played a part in the assaults because an assault a common assault doesn't even have to cause injury because I have read the definition of common assault but you played a part in this because you facilitated Mrs. Brown in what she was doing. You got the weapons and I use that word deliberately because they were weapons that she used against the child. You got them for her. You provided them.

You held the child on occasion and on occasion you beat the child herself for no reason and it is not an excuse to say that you beat the child to prevent her from being beaten by somebody else. So that you assaulted that child not on a pretext or not even on the suggestion that she had done something wrong but rather because beatings apparently were the normal thing in your household and you were the father of the household.

Now I'd be very clear that the evidence of Sandra's brother and sister who gave evidence here in court actually confirms what Sandra has said, not altogether, but in part and I suspect now that they having a continuing relationship with you and probably

Sandra Mae Brown

feeling a great deal of sympathy and pity for you in the state that you're in here before the court, I suspect in their own minds have minimized your role in all this and I can't blame them or fault them for that. They too had extremely difficult childhoods because the conditions in that home were appalling and I don't think anybody can gainsay that. That is pretty obvious from all the evidence which has been heard.

But you too Mr. Brown were a part of these assaults nd you yourself committed some if not, some but not all, of these assaults and I have no doubt in that. It is again not a case of weighing reasonable doubt. It has been clearly proven by the evidence that has been brought before the court substantiated on by different witnesses, not just Sandra herself, but even by your own evidence and the evidence of the other children and confirmed by the medical evidence which has been filed with the court and from which I have read. So Mr. Brown I find you guilty also of the charge of common assault which has been laid against you.

*

Father was sentenced to less than two years, as I go on living a lifetime of pain, not commuted, for his crimes and hers.

When both parents got out of jail, I was once again confronted with my family's rejection. My sisters threw welcome home parties for the mother who had almost killed me. I returned to New Brunswick again feeling alone and unwanted.

With the help of my best friend, Gwen Nicholas, I have since those days become a stronger person. Gwen and her family have been my rock. They have stood by my side through it all. Gwen and I met in the late 1980s and bonded like sisters from day one. I will always be grateful for the love and support she has shown me over the years and for the long, sleepless nights she spent with me as we cried together. I can never begin to repay her for the love and care she showed my children when I was reliving some of the roughest times in my life. I can honestly say I would not be here today to tell this story without her love and support. Thanks to

174

Gwen and my children, today I am my own person. I've learned to let go of the past and to cherish every day.

I have no regrets about coming forward with my story. I wish that my siblings had been supportive, but you can't pick your family. My only regret is that I wish I had spoken out earlier. But I do believe there is a time for all things. I feel this is my time and space that God has given me to share my story. My hope is to help other victims of abuse with this testament.

I have a new life now. If I could leave any message for the public, it would be, simply, Do not hurt children.

They are society's most priceless possession. Their safety and well-being should be a community's first priority. Be aware of what is going on in your community. We owe that to the children around us.

Today, I would give anything just to be able to share with my readers some happy memories of my childhood. But try as I may, no happy thoughts come to mind. I often fantasize about what my life would have been like if I had been given two loving parents or not been forced to return to them. I rail against a system that gives parents second, third, and fourth chances without checking to see what is really happening in that household. If someone had spoken up about my obvious neglect and abuse—my grandparents, the lady next door, a priest, the grocer, a teacher—my life would have been so very different.

The child who lived within me all those years is now free through my writing. But the memories of that little girl's anguish will always live within my mind. Over the years I have learned to deal with my past. I am now ready to speak to the world about the subject of child abuse, with hopes of one day regaining the love of my siblings. Until her recent death I also yearned for an apology from my mother for the way she treated me.

I'll always remember my mother's words, repeated over and over down through the years, "I'll give you marks to carry to your grave." My scars stand clearly for the world to see. Sometimes when I look in the mirror, I still see that dirty, wide-eyed little child looking back at me from the glass. I will always remember the pain. The scars are there to remind me.

I am reminded every day that it should not hurt to be a child. No one should have to feel guilt or shame for being born. No one should bear scars inflicted by the hands of their own parents. No one should be held as a prisoner and denied food and water. Who gives parents the right to act like cold-hearted prison guards while a child cries and prays to die between the cold, dirty walls of a lonely, dark room?

For many years, I thought of myself as a nobody, a cipher. I still have to remind myself every day that God spared my life for a purpose. Maybe I can help someone else in pain. Maybe my story of survival will encourage someone to believe in him/herself again.

I am far from saying that it's all behind me yet. But with God's love and guidance, I am on my way to a happier life. I hope that with this book I will touch many more lives as well. The love of God and being strong carried me through the trauma years. Believe in yourself and His helping hand will also carry you!

Sharing my story has been one of the hardest things I have ever done. Telling it has brought back all the hurt and isolation that marked my childhood. But I am proud to have finally told my story and now feel that I am ready to move on. I have learned to take life one day at a time and never, when looking back into the past, to linger there. I've learned to speak up only because I believe that, in the end, the things that we hold inside are what make us victims.

I encourage others who have been the victims of abuse— at the hands of a parent, a relative, a coach, a neighbour, a teacher, a member of the clergy, or anyone else—to speak up. Don't let abuse continue. By telling your story, you may save the life of another child.

Mommy & Daddy,

I am sorry. But you see, I tried to stop you, By crying out in pain, That I wanted you to stop.

When I told you over and over again how sorry I was, You wouldn't hear me. When I looked at you with tears running down my face, I wanted you to stop.

I tried hard to do my best, But you never approved. You never once thought to stop.

So you see, Mommy & Daddy, The day has come for me to get help.

Though I sit and cry as they take you away, I'm sorry, I love you, I can't stop.

Printed in Canada